DNSSEC: Protecting the Domain Name System

James Relington

DEDICATION

To those who seek knowledge, inspiration, and new perspectives—
may this book be a companion on your journey, a spark for curiosity,
and a reminder that every page turned is a step toward discovery.

AKNOWLEDGEMENTS

I would like to express my deepest gratitude to everyone who contributed to the creation of this book. To my colleagues and mentors, your insights and expertise have been invaluable. A special thank you to my family and friends for their unwavering support and encouragement throughout this journey.

Introduction to DNSSEC

The Domain Name System Security Extensions, or DNSSEC, is a suite of protocols designed to secure information provided by the Domain Name System (DNS), which is one of the foundational components of the modern Internet. DNS itself acts as the phonebook of the internet, translating human-readable domain names like example.com into IP addresses that computers use to locate one another. This seemingly simple service is essential to the operation of virtually every online service, from websites to email and countless other applications. However, when DNS was originally designed in the early 1980s, security was not a primary concern. Its creators assumed that the network would operate within a trusted environment. As the internet grew exponentially and became globally accessible, this assumption no longer held true.

Without security mechanisms in place, DNS is vulnerable to a range of attacks, including cache poisoning and man-in-the-middle attacks.

These attacks can redirect users to malicious websites without their knowledge, compromise data integrity, or enable the interception of sensitive information. For instance, a user attempting to visit a legitimate banking website might be silently redirected to a fraudulent page, where attackers can harvest login credentials and other personal information. The consequences of such attacks can range from individual identity theft to large-scale breaches affecting millions of users.

DNSSEC was introduced as a solution to these growing threats, adding a critical layer of security to the DNS infrastructure. It does so by enabling DNS responses to be cryptographically signed. This means that when a DNS resolver queries for a domain name, it can verify that the response it receives actually comes from the authoritative source and has not been tampered with during transit. The cornerstone of DNSSEC lies in public key cryptography, where a set of private and public keys are used to sign and validate DNS records.

While DNSSEC does not encrypt the actual DNS data or hide the domain name being queried, it ensures that the data has not been altered, spoofed, or forged. The integrity of DNS records is guaranteed by digital signatures that accompany them. When a resolver receives a DNS response, it also receives a signature, which it can verify against the public key published in the DNSKEY record of the authoritative zone. If the signature is valid, the resolver knows that the data is authentic and has not been modified.

The implementation of DNSSEC involves multiple new resource records in the DNS protocol. These include DNSKEY, RRSIG, NSEC, NSEC3, and DS records. Each plays a crucial role in ensuring the proper functioning of DNSSEC and the integrity of DNS queries and responses. Among these, the DNSKEY record stores the public key used for signature verification, and the RRSIG record contains the digital signature corresponding to DNS records. DS records help establish a chain of trust between parent and child zones, which is vital for maintaining trustworthiness across the hierarchical structure of the DNS.

One of the most significant features of DNSSEC is the concept of a "chain of trust." This chain begins with a trust anchor, typically the root zone of the DNS, which is trusted implicitly. Each zone in the DNS hierarchy signs its records and provides DS records to its parent zone. In this way, a recursive resolver can start from the root zone and verify the authenticity of each link in the chain until it reaches the target domain. If any link is broken or unverifiable, the resolver will treat the data as untrustworthy and, depending on its configuration, may refuse to resolve the domain name altogether.

Despite its benefits, the deployment of DNSSEC has not been universal. Many organizations, Internet Service Providers (ISPs), and domain registrars have been slow to adopt it due to perceived complexity, resource requirements, and operational risks. Managing DNSSEC involves careful handling of cryptographic keys, timely key rollovers, and ensuring that signatures are always current and properly validated. Mistakes in implementation can result in domain outages or resolution failures, which dissuades some administrators from enabling DNSSEC in their environments.

Nevertheless, DNSSEC adoption has steadily increased, supported by industry groups, governments, and security advocates who recognize the importance of securing the global DNS infrastructure. Major top-level domains (TLDs) such as .com, .org, and many country-code TLDs have signed their zones with DNSSEC, and large-scale DNS resolvers like Google Public DNS and Cloudflare's 1.1.1.1 service perform DNSSEC validation by default. These steps are pivotal in fostering a safer internet ecosystem where users can trust that they are accessing legitimate resources and not falling victim to DNS-based attacks.

As cyber threats continue to evolve, the importance of DNSSEC becomes even more pronounced. The modern internet economy relies heavily on trust, and ensuring the integrity of DNS data is fundamental to maintaining that trust. The introduction of DNSSEC marks a significant milestone in securing internet infrastructure, but it is only part of a broader effort to protect online communications. In this book, we will explore in depth how DNSSEC operates, how it can be implemented and managed effectively, and how it integrates with other security protocols to create a robust and resilient defense against DNS-related threats.

The Evolution of DNS

The Domain Name System, commonly referred to as DNS, is one of the most critical and enduring components of the internet's infrastructure. It functions as the distributed, hierarchical system that translates human-readable domain names into IP addresses, allowing users to access websites, send emails, and use a variety of other online services without having to memorize numerical addresses. The journey of DNS from its inception to its present form reflects the growth and complexities of the modern internet, shaped by technological advancement, user demands, and the growing awareness of security and performance needs.

The origins of DNS date back to the early days of ARPANET, the precursor to today's internet. In the late 1960s and early 1970s, computers on ARPANET communicated using hostnames mapped to IP addresses. These mappings were maintained manually in a single text file known as HOSTS.TXT, which was centrally managed by the Stanford Research Institute's Network Information Center (SRI-NIC). As the network grew, distributing and updating this file became increasingly cumbersome and unsustainable. Each time a new host was added to the network, the file had to be updated and redistributed to every participating computer. This manual process led to delays, inconsistencies, and inefficiencies.

By the early 1980s, it was clear that a scalable, automated system was needed to handle the growing number of hosts on the internet. In 1983, Paul Mockapetris introduced the Domain Name System in RFCs 882 and 883, which were later refined by RFCs 1034 and 1035. This new system replaced the static HOSTS.TXT file with a dynamic, distributed database, capable of handling the exponentially increasing demand for name-to-address resolution. DNS divided the namespace into a hierarchy of domains, beginning with the root zone at the top, followed by top-level domains (TLDs) such as .com, .edu, .gov, and country-code TLDs like .uk and .jp, and further down into second-level and subdomains.

This hierarchical structure was revolutionary because it delegated authority over different parts of the namespace to different organizations. The root zone is managed by a set of root servers, while individual TLDs are administered by registries, and organizations can manage their own domains and subdomains. This delegation of authority made DNS highly scalable and allowed the internet to expand rapidly throughout the 1980s and 1990s. With the rise of the World Wide Web in the 1990s, DNS became indispensable to everyday internet use, facilitating the user-friendly experience of accessing websites by typing easy-to-remember domain names instead of numerical IP addresses.

Over time, DNS underwent several technical improvements to enhance its functionality and efficiency. Caching was introduced to reduce the load on authoritative servers and improve response times for end users. Recursive resolvers could store previously queried DNS records for a defined period, serving them from memory instead of repeatedly querying the authoritative source. Load balancing techniques were also adopted, with multiple IP addresses assigned to a single domain to distribute traffic across servers and improve resilience and performance.

As the internet matured, so did the threats against DNS. The original DNS design did not incorporate security as a core feature, leaving it vulnerable to attacks such as DNS spoofing and cache poisoning. In a DNS spoofing attack, a malicious actor intercepts or manipulates DNS queries to return false IP addresses, redirecting users to fraudulent websites. The growing incidence of these attacks in the late 1990s and early 2000s highlighted the need for enhanced security mechanisms within the DNS protocol.

At the same time, the global adoption of the internet brought new requirements for DNS to support internationalized domain names (IDNs), allowing domain names to include non-ASCII characters and support a broader range of languages and scripts. This helped make the internet more inclusive and accessible to users around the world.

To address the mounting security concerns, DNS Security Extensions (DNSSEC) were introduced, adding a layer of cryptographic validation to DNS responses. DNSSEC provided a way for resolvers to verify that the information they received was authentic and had not been tampered with during transit. The deployment of DNSSEC began slowly, with the root zone finally being signed in 2010. Since then, adoption has expanded, although not universally, as DNSSEC requires significant changes to DNS operations and ongoing maintenance of cryptographic keys.

Another major development in the evolution of DNS was the introduction of new TLDs. Originally limited to a small set of generic and country-code TLDs, the DNS landscape expanded dramatically with the creation of hundreds of new generic TLDs (gTLDs) under ICANN's new gTLD program launched in 2012. Domains such as .app, .blog, .guru, and countless others became available, diversifying the namespace and creating new branding opportunities for businesses and individuals.

The advent of DNS over HTTPS (DoH) and DNS over TLS (DoT) marked the latest phase of DNS's evolution. These protocols encrypt DNS queries and responses, protecting user privacy and preventing eavesdropping or manipulation by third parties. While DoH and DoT enhance privacy, they also introduce operational challenges and debates about the balance between security, user control, and network management.

Today, DNS continues to evolve alongside the internet itself. With the rise of edge computing, content delivery networks, and the Internet of Things (IoT), DNS has adapted to support billions of connected devices and services worldwide. The increasing reliance on cloud services and distributed architectures has further highlighted the critical role of DNS in ensuring both availability and performance.

From its humble beginnings as a simple static text file to its modern role as a globally distributed, secure, and resilient system, DNS has undergone profound transformations. Its evolution reflects not only the rapid growth of the internet but also the constant need to adapt to emerging technological and security challenges. As DNS continues to advance, it remains a pillar of internet functionality, shaping how users connect, interact, and trust the online world.

Vulnerabilities in Traditional DNS

The original design of the Domain Name System, while revolutionary in enabling the internet to grow and scale, was developed at a time when security threats were not a central concern. The designers of DNS prioritized efficiency, scalability, and reliability in a trusted environment where bad actors were not anticipated. As the internet became a global and public network, however, the lack of built-in security mechanisms in traditional DNS began to expose severe vulnerabilities that could be exploited by malicious parties. These weaknesses have led to various attack vectors that compromise the integrity, availability, and confidentiality of DNS operations.

One of the most significant vulnerabilities in traditional DNS is cache poisoning. DNS cache poisoning, also known as DNS spoofing, occurs when an attacker introduces false information into a resolver's cache, causing the resolver to return incorrect responses to DNS queries. Once poisoned, the resolver will continue to serve the malicious DNS data until the time-to-live (TTL) value expires or the cache is manually cleared. Attackers exploit this vulnerability to redirect users to fraudulent websites without their knowledge. For instance, a user trying to visit their bank's legitimate website might unknowingly be directed to a phishing page controlled by the attacker, where sensitive information such as login credentials and personal data can be stolen. This type of attack is particularly dangerous because it undermines the implicit trust users place in DNS, leaving them exposed to fraud and cybercrime.

Another common vulnerability is the lack of data origin authentication in traditional DNS. In the standard DNS query-response model, there is no built-in mechanism for resolvers to verify the authenticity of the data they receive. DNS responses can be intercepted and modified in transit by attackers performing man-in-the-middle (MITM) attacks. By inserting themselves between a client and a DNS resolver or between a resolver and an authoritative server, attackers can manipulate DNS queries and responses to their advantage. Without any form of cryptographic signature to verify the source, the resolver or client has no means to determine if the received DNS data has been tampered with.

Traditional DNS is also susceptible to amplification attacks, which are commonly used in Distributed Denial of Service (DDoS) attacks. In a DNS amplification attack, an attacker sends DNS queries with a spoofed source IP address, typically belonging to a targeted victim, to open DNS resolvers. The responses sent back to the victim are significantly larger than the initial queries, resulting in an amplification effect that overwhelms the victim's network or services. Because DNS uses the UDP transport protocol, which does not establish a connection before sending data, it is particularly vulnerable to source address spoofing. Attackers exploit this to reflect and amplify traffic toward their targets, causing widespread outages and service disruptions.

Another issue inherent in traditional DNS is zone transfer leakage. DNS uses zone transfers, specifically AXFR (full zone transfer) and IXFR (incremental zone transfer), to replicate DNS databases between primary and secondary servers. If improperly configured, these transfers can be performed by unauthorized parties, giving attackers access to the entire DNS zone file. The zone file contains valuable information about the structure of a domain, including subdomains, IP addresses, and mail servers. This data can be leveraged by attackers during reconnaissance activities to map an organization's network and identify potential targets for further exploitation.

DNS also lacks protection against enumeration techniques, such as DNS zone walking. In environments where NSEC records are used without additional obfuscation techniques like NSEC3, attackers can enumerate all the existing domain names within a zone. By performing repeated queries for non-existent domain names and analyzing the NSEC records returned, attackers can gather a list of valid domain names that may expose internal services or resources not intended for public access.

Replay attacks pose another risk within traditional DNS operations. Because DNS queries and responses are often repeated and cached across various resolvers, an attacker can capture a legitimate DNS response and later replay it in a different context, potentially misleading systems that depend on up-to-date DNS data. The stateless nature of DNS transactions and the absence of cryptographic timestamps or unique transaction identifiers in traditional DNS increase the risk of these types of attacks.

Furthermore, DNS suffers from privacy concerns as it does not encrypt the queries or responses. This allows third parties, including ISPs, network administrators, or malicious actors, to monitor DNS traffic and gain insight into user behavior. DNS queries reveal which domains users are attempting to access, which can be valuable for tracking, surveillance, or targeted attacks. The exposure of DNS traffic in plaintext has led to calls for greater confidentiality mechanisms within the protocol.

The reliance on the UDP protocol also means DNS is prone to packet forgery and interception. UDP's lack of session establishment and verification creates a situation where an attacker can inject forged packets that mimic legitimate DNS responses. Timing plays a critical role here, as attackers aim to have their forged response arrive before the legitimate response from the authoritative server. If successful, the forged response will be cached by the resolver and served to clients, leading to potential traffic redirection and compromise.

These vulnerabilities collectively illustrate how the core design of traditional DNS, while efficient and scalable, fails to address modern security threats. The growth of the internet into an open and often hostile environment has exposed these weaknesses, making DNS a frequent target for attackers. The increasing reliance on DNS for essential services and the proliferation of cybercrime have made it clear that enhancements to DNS are necessary to protect users and organizations from these risks.

The response to these vulnerabilities has been the development of security-focused extensions like DNSSEC, as well as the introduction of privacy-preserving protocols such as DNS over HTTPS and DNS over TLS. However, despite these advancements, a significant portion of DNS traffic on the internet still operates without these protections, leaving millions of users exposed to the inherent weaknesses of traditional DNS. The ongoing transition toward more secure DNS practices is therefore a crucial element in strengthening the resilience of the internet against an ever-evolving landscape of cyber threats.

The Need for DNS Security

The Domain Name System is the backbone of how users interact with the internet. Every time a user types a web address into their browser, sends an email, or connects to an online service, DNS is responsible for translating human-readable domain names into machine-readable IP addresses. This invisible yet vital process occurs billions of times each day, allowing seamless navigation through the vast network of interconnected systems that form the modern internet. Despite its critical role, DNS was never designed with strong security principles in mind. When it was first created, the internet was a much smaller and more trusted environment. Over time, as the internet expanded to become a global infrastructure supporting commerce, communication, and essential services, the limitations and vulnerabilities of DNS have become more apparent and increasingly exploited.

The absence of security in traditional DNS leaves both users and organizations exposed to a variety of cyber threats. Cybercriminals, hacktivists, and state-sponsored actors all recognize DNS as a high-value target due to its central role in connecting users to digital resources. Successful attacks against DNS can lead to severe consequences, including data breaches, service outages, fraud, and the erosion of trust between users and online platforms. As the internet has become more integrated into every aspect of modern life, securing DNS has shifted from being a technical preference to a necessity for the protection of businesses, governments, and end users.

One of the core reasons DNS security is essential is the rise of DNS-based attacks, particularly DNS cache poisoning and spoofing. These attacks allow adversaries to intercept and manipulate DNS queries, redirecting users to malicious destinations without their awareness. This is especially problematic because users typically rely on DNS behind the scenes, rarely interacting directly with the system or considering the possibility that a query might be compromised. When users are silently redirected to counterfeit websites or rogue servers, attackers can harvest sensitive information such as usernames, passwords, credit card details, and personal data. The lack of data authenticity and integrity in traditional DNS means that once a resolver is compromised, every user depending on that resolver can be exposed to harm.

The consequences of DNS insecurity extend beyond financial loss and identity theft. DNS has also been exploited in large-scale Distributed Denial of Service attacks, where attackers abuse the protocol's design to flood networks and services with overwhelming traffic. By leveraging open resolvers and the amplification properties of DNS, attackers can magnify their impact, crippling websites, applications, and critical online services. Such attacks have not only targeted private companies but also governments, financial institutions, healthcare providers, and other vital sectors. The fallout from these disruptions affects public confidence, economic stability, and, in some cases, national security.

The growing sophistication of threat actors has further emphasized the need for DNS security. Cybercriminals are no longer limited to basic attacks but employ complex tactics, combining DNS vulnerabilities with other techniques such as phishing, malware delivery, and command-and-control communications. Many types of malware use DNS to evade detection, embedding their traffic within normal-looking DNS queries and responses. These covert channels can bypass traditional security mechanisms such as firewalls and intrusion detection systems, allowing attackers to establish persistent access to compromised systems. Without secure DNS, organizations face increased difficulty in identifying and mitigating these advanced threats.

Another factor driving the urgency for DNS security is the global shift toward digital transformation. The proliferation of online services, cloud computing, and remote work has led to a broader attack surface, increasing reliance on DNS across diverse environments. Organizations now depend on DNS not only for public-facing websites but also for internal applications, remote employee access, and cloud-based infrastructure. Insecure DNS undermines the foundation upon which these services are built, making them susceptible to interception, redirection, or denial of service.

The protection of privacy is another compelling reason to prioritize DNS security. Traditional DNS queries are transmitted in plaintext, allowing anyone with access to the network path — such as internet service providers, Wi-Fi hotspot operators, or malicious insiders — to monitor and log users' browsing habits. This surveillance can be used for commercial exploitation, government monitoring, or criminal purposes. In an age where data privacy is a growing concern, particularly in light of regulations such as the General Data Protection Regulation (GDPR), leaving DNS traffic exposed runs counter to global efforts to safeguard user information and uphold fundamental rights.

From a business perspective, DNS insecurity can also result in reputational damage and legal liability. When customers are harmed due to attacks made possible by weak DNS protections, companies may face public backlash, regulatory scrutiny, and costly legal proceedings. Beyond direct financial losses, organizations risk losing customer trust and market credibility, which can take years to rebuild. In competitive industries where brand reputation is critical, the inability to demonstrate a commitment to DNS security can result in long-term business setbacks.

Governments and international organizations have recognized the importance of securing DNS and have called for widespread adoption of standards such as DNS Security Extensions (DNSSEC). DNSSEC mitigates many of the risks inherent in traditional DNS by introducing cryptographic signatures that verify the authenticity and integrity of DNS data. While DNSSEC does not encrypt queries, it ensures that DNS responses have not been altered in transit, effectively preventing cache poisoning and spoofing attacks. Furthermore, the emergence of DNS over HTTPS (DoH) and DNS over TLS (DoT) has addressed privacy concerns by encrypting DNS queries, shielding them from eavesdropping and tampering.

The internet has become an essential utility, supporting modern economies, public services, and everyday life. As such, the security of DNS has become a cornerstone of global cybersecurity efforts. The growing interconnectedness of devices, services, and users means that the repercussions of DNS vulnerabilities can cascade quickly, affecting not only individual organizations but also entire sectors and regions. The stakes are too high to ignore. As attackers continuously evolve and adapt, so too must the security measures safeguarding the DNS infrastructure. Strengthening DNS security is not just a technical enhancement; it is a critical step toward ensuring a safer, more trustworthy, and resilient internet for everyone.

DNSSEC Fundamentals

DNS Security Extensions, or DNSSEC, is a collection of protocols designed to address the fundamental security weaknesses inherent in the original Domain Name System. The core purpose of DNSSEC is to protect the integrity and authenticity of DNS data. Traditional DNS was built for a time when trust on the internet could be assumed. As the internet evolved into an open and often hostile environment, DNS became a prime target for attackers. DNSSEC emerged to address these vulnerabilities by introducing cryptographic signatures that ensure DNS responses cannot be forged or altered undetected. The fundamental principle of DNSSEC is that every response to a DNS query should be verifiable and provably authentic.

At the heart of DNSSEC is the use of public key cryptography. Every zone that deploys DNSSEC generates a pair of cryptographic keys: a private key used to create digital signatures and a public key that is published for others to use to verify those signatures. When a DNS zone is signed with DNSSEC, each DNS record set in the zone is accompanied by a digital signature. This signature is created using the private key and is stored in a special resource record called the RRSIG (Resource Record Signature). When a DNS resolver queries a DNSSEC-protected zone, it receives not only the DNS records it requested but also the corresponding RRSIG records. The resolver then uses the public key, published in a DNSKEY record, to verify that the signature matches the data and that it has not been tampered with in transit.

A critical concept in DNSSEC is the chain of trust. DNS is inherently hierarchical, with the root zone at the top, followed by top-level domains, second-level domains, and so forth. DNSSEC leverages this hierarchy by establishing cryptographic links between zones. For example, a top-level domain such as .com will sign a hash of a second-level domain's public key in a record called a Delegation Signer (DS) record. This DS record is placed in the parent zone, linking the child zone's DNSKEY record to the parent zone. This relationship is established all the way from the root zone down to individual domains. A resolver begins at a trusted starting point, known as the trust anchor, which is typically the root zone's public key. From there, it follows the chain of DS records and DNSKEY records to verify the authenticity of the DNS data. If any link in this chain is broken or missing, the resolver will treat the DNS data as untrustworthy.

DNSSEC introduces several new DNS resource record types that work together to provide security. In addition to DNSKEY, RRSIG, and DS records, DNSSEC also uses NSEC and NSEC3 records to provide authenticated denial of existence. When a resolver queries a non-existent domain name, a signed NSEC or NSEC3 record is returned to prove that no such name exists in the zone. Without this mechanism, an attacker could exploit the absence of signed responses to forge non-existent domain responses. NSEC records list the next existing name in the zone, which can lead to zone enumeration, where an attacker discovers all domain names in a zone. NSEC3 was introduced as an enhancement to mitigate this risk by hashing domain names, making it harder to conduct zone-walking attacks.

Another fundamental aspect of DNSSEC is key management. Zones often use two types of keys: the Key Signing Key (KSK) and the Zone Signing Key (ZSK). The KSK is used to sign the DNSKEY record set, while the ZSK is used to sign all other zone data. This separation of duties helps with operational management and security. The KSK is generally rolled over less frequently and is the key that is submitted to the parent zone in the form of a DS record. The ZSK is rotated more regularly to limit the exposure of the key in case of compromise. Proper key management is essential, as losing a private key or failing to roll keys correctly can result in DNS resolution failures.

Resolvers must be configured to validate DNSSEC signatures. A validating resolver will check the digital signatures of DNS responses against the public keys in the DNSKEY records, following the chain of trust up to the root trust anchor. If any signature fails validation, the resolver treats the response as bogus and typically refuses to resolve the domain, protecting the user from potentially malicious data. For DNSSEC to function effectively, both authoritative servers and resolvers must be DNSSEC-aware and properly configured to sign, serve, and validate DNSSEC-protected data.

While DNSSEC significantly improves the security posture of DNS, it is important to note that DNSSEC does not provide confidentiality. DNS queries and responses are still transmitted in plaintext and can be observed by intermediaries. DNSSEC focuses on ensuring that the DNS data is authentic and has not been altered, but it does not encrypt the communication between client and server. To address confidentiality concerns, protocols such as DNS over HTTPS (DoH) and DNS over TLS (DoT) are used in conjunction with DNSSEC.

Deploying DNSSEC can be complex and requires careful planning and ongoing maintenance. Administrators must ensure that zone files are properly signed, keys are securely stored and regularly rotated, and DS records are accurately published in the parent zone. Additionally, DNSSEC increases the size of DNS responses due to the inclusion of cryptographic signatures and additional records, which may necessitate adjustments to resolver and firewall configurations to handle larger UDP packets or fallback to TCP more gracefully.

Despite these operational considerations, DNSSEC provides a robust framework to defend against common DNS attacks such as cache poisoning and man-in-the-middle attacks. By introducing cryptographic validation into DNS responses, DNSSEC establishes a higher level of trust in the resolution process, making it significantly harder for attackers to inject false information into DNS lookups.

The implementation of DNSSEC across the internet has steadily grown, particularly among top-level domains and major service providers. As adoption continues to expand, DNSSEC forms a crucial component in the broader movement toward a more secure and resilient internet infrastructure. It strengthens the DNS layer, ensuring that users can trust that the domain names they resolve truly map to legitimate and intended IP addresses, creating a safer environment for global communication and commerce.

How DNSSEC Works

DNSSEC adds a layer of security to the Domain Name System by using cryptographic signatures to ensure the authenticity and integrity of

DNS data. The core principle of DNSSEC is that every response from a DNS server should be verifiable by the recipient to confirm that it comes from an authoritative source and has not been altered during transit. This is achieved through a combination of public key cryptography, digital signatures, and a hierarchical system of trust that extends from the root of the DNS down to individual domains.

When a DNS zone is configured to use DNSSEC, the zone administrator generates a pair of cryptographic keys. One key is private and is used to sign DNS records, while the other is public and is published within the zone as a DNSKEY record. Every set of DNS records, known as a Resource Record Set or RRset, is signed using the private key. The resulting digital signature is stored in an RRSIG record, which is then included alongside the RRset in DNS responses. When a recursive resolver queries the DNS for information, it receives not only the requested data but also the RRSIG signature. The resolver can then use the public key from the DNSKEY record to verify the signature, ensuring that the data has not been tampered with since it was signed by the authoritative server.

The verification process relies on a hierarchical trust model. At the top of the DNS hierarchy is the root zone, which has its own cryptographic key pair. The public part of this key pair, known as the root trust anchor, is widely distributed and configured in validating resolvers around the world. From the root zone, the chain of trust extends down through each level of the DNS hierarchy. For example, when a top-level domain such as .org is signed, the root zone contains a Delegation Signer (DS) record that points to the .org zone's DNSKEY. The .org zone, in turn, may contain DS records for second-level domains, such as example.org, which have their own DNSKEY records. This creates an unbroken path of cryptographic signatures from the root down to the individual domain name.

When a resolver validates a DNSSEC-signed response, it begins at the trust anchor and follows this chain of trust step-by-step. It starts by checking the DS record in the parent zone, then retrieves the corresponding DNSKEY record in the child zone, and continues this process until it reaches the zone that signed the RRset in question. If any link in this chain fails verification, the resolver will treat the DNS data as invalid and may refuse to return an answer to the client, thereby protecting the user from potentially malicious or corrupted data.

DNSSEC not only signs positive answers to queries but also provides authenticated denial of existence. When a resolver queries for a non-existent domain, the authoritative server responds with either an NSEC or NSEC3 record. These records cryptographically prove that the domain name does not exist in the zone. NSEC records do this by providing the names of the next valid records in lexicographical order, demonstrating that the queried name falls between two valid names and is therefore absent. NSEC3 enhances this by using hashed domain names to prevent attackers from easily enumerating all valid names within a zone, addressing privacy concerns associated with NSEC.

Another important element of how DNSSEC works is the distinction between the Key Signing Key (KSK) and the Zone Signing Key (ZSK). The KSK is responsible for signing the DNSKEY record set, while the ZSK is used to sign all other zone records. This separation allows for more flexible and secure key management. The KSK, being critical to the chain of trust, is typically stored more securely and rolled over less frequently. The ZSK, which signs more data, is rotated more regularly to limit its exposure in case of compromise.

Resolvers must be DNSSEC-aware to perform signature validation. When configured with the root trust anchor, a validating resolver will automatically attempt to validate DNSSEC signatures when querying DNS records. If a resolver encounters a zone that is not signed with DNSSEC, it will proceed as it would under traditional DNS, returning unsigned data. However, if a resolver queries a signed zone and cannot validate the data, it will return a security error rather than forwarding untrusted information to the client. This behavior prevents users from being redirected to forged destinations by attackers attempting to poison the DNS cache or conduct man-in-the-middle attacks.

Because DNSSEC increases the size of DNS responses due to the inclusion of RRSIG, DNSKEY, and other related records, the protocol relies on the Extension Mechanisms for DNS (EDNS0) to allow DNS messages larger than the traditional 512-byte limit. In many cases, this necessitates the use of TCP fallback when UDP packets are truncated due to size constraints. Therefore, DNSSEC deployment also requires careful attention to firewall and network device configurations to ensure that large DNS messages and TCP traffic are permitted.

The process of maintaining DNSSEC involves regular key rollovers and resigning of zone data. Zone administrators must periodically replace their ZSK and, on a less frequent schedule, their KSK. Each time a key is rolled over, the zone must be re-signed, and the new DS record must be updated in the parent zone to maintain the chain of trust. Automating key rollovers and monitoring for errors is crucial to prevent service disruptions. An improperly managed rollover or a missing DS record can break DNS resolution for a domain, causing outages until the issue is resolved.

DNSSEC also operates in tandem with other security protocols. For example, DNSSEC is essential for the functioning of DANE (DNS-based Authentication of Named Entities), which allows services such as email and TLS certificates to leverage DNSSEC for additional security assurances. By binding cryptographic certificates or public keys to DNS records, DANE can provide a trust mechanism that is resistant to attacks against traditional certificate authorities.

By leveraging public key infrastructure, digital signatures, and a hierarchical trust model, DNSSEC fundamentally changes how DNS data is validated. It transforms DNS from an inherently insecure protocol into a system where authenticity and integrity can be assured. This makes DNSSEC a cornerstone of modern internet security, providing essential protection against tampering and redirection attacks that have plagued DNS for decades. While deployment challenges remain, the way DNSSEC works is a powerful example of how cryptography can strengthen critical internet infrastructure.

Public Key Cryptography in DNSSEC

Public key cryptography is the foundation on which DNSSEC operates, ensuring that DNS data can be verified as authentic and unaltered. At its core, public key cryptography is a system that uses a pair of cryptographic keys: one public and one private. The private key is kept secret and is used to sign data, while the public key is distributed widely and is used to verify the authenticity of the signature. In the context of DNSSEC, this mechanism ensures that any DNS response can be checked against a known public key to confirm that it was signed by the legitimate authority for that zone.

In traditional DNS, when a resolver queries for a domain name, the authoritative server returns an answer without any cryptographic proof. Anyone positioned between the resolver and the authoritative server could potentially alter the response without detection. Public key cryptography eliminates this weakness by enabling the authoritative server to sign its DNS data with its private key before sending it out. The resolver, upon receiving the data, uses the corresponding public key to verify that the signature is valid. If the verification process succeeds, the resolver can trust that the data has not been modified in transit and originates from the rightful owner of the domain.

DNSSEC utilizes specific DNS record types to facilitate this process. The DNSKEY record contains the public key used to verify digital signatures on DNS data. Each zone that implements DNSSEC will have one or more DNSKEY records published within it. These keys are then used to verify the RRSIG records, which contain the digital signatures for DNS resource record sets. The digital signature is created by applying a private key to a cryptographic hash of the DNS data, resulting in a unique signature that can only be correctly verified using the matching public key. This process is crucial because it ensures that if even a single bit of the DNS data were altered, the signature would no longer be valid, and the resolver would detect the tampering.

An essential part of DNSSEC's use of public key cryptography is its hierarchical trust model. The DNS is organized in a tree-like structure, with the root zone at the top, followed by top-level domains such as .com or .net, and then second-level domains like example.com. Each zone signs its own data with its private key and publishes its public key in the DNSKEY record. The parent zone, such as .com, then creates a DS record (Delegation Signer) for each child zone. The DS record contains a hash of the child zone's DNSKEY record and is itself signed by the parent's private key. This chaining of signatures forms the so-called chain of trust. When a resolver receives DNS data, it can start at the root trust anchor, which is a known and widely distributed public key, and then validate each level of the hierarchy step-by-step by checking these cryptographically linked records.

DNSSEC makes use of two types of keys: the Key Signing Key (KSK) and the Zone Signing Key (ZSK). The KSK is used exclusively to sign the DNSKEY record set, while the ZSK is used to sign the rest of the zone data. Both of these keys are pairs of public and private keys. Separating these two types of keys allows for more secure and manageable key operations. The KSK, for instance, is typically rolled over less frequently because it forms the link between the zone and its parent in the DNS hierarchy. The ZSK, on the other hand, is used more frequently to sign all other resource record sets and may be rotated more often to minimize exposure.

The algorithms used for public key cryptography in DNSSEC are based on well-established cryptographic standards. The most commonly used algorithms include RSA (Rivest-Shamir-Adleman) and ECDSA (Elliptic Curve Digital Signature Algorithm). RSA, historically the most widely adopted, uses longer keys and is generally considered more computationally intensive. ECDSA, on the other hand, provides the same level of security with shorter key lengths, which reduces computational overhead and results in smaller DNS messages. The choice of algorithm affects not only the security posture but also the performance of DNSSEC-enabled zones, particularly in environments where minimizing packet sizes and improving efficiency are critical.

Key management is an ongoing operational responsibility when using public key cryptography in DNSSEC. Private keys must be stored securely to prevent unauthorized access or compromise. If a private key is stolen or leaked, an attacker could use it to create valid-looking DNS signatures and undermine the trustworthiness of the zone. Administrators must also periodically perform key rollovers, generating new key pairs and updating the relevant DNS records. When rolling over a KSK, for example, the DS record in the parent zone must also be updated to point to the hash of the new public key. This process must be carefully coordinated to avoid breaking the chain of trust and causing DNS resolution failures.

Public key cryptography also introduces additional computational overhead. Signing DNS records with private keys and verifying signatures with public keys require processing power and can add latency to the DNS resolution process. However, modern hardware and optimized DNS software mitigate much of this overhead, and the security benefits of DNSSEC far outweigh these performance considerations. The increasing use of efficient algorithms like ECDSA further reduces the computational burden while maintaining strong cryptographic guarantees.

Resolvers that support DNSSEC must be able to handle the public key cryptography operations involved in signature verification. They must also be configured with a valid root trust anchor, which is the public key of the root zone's KSK. This anchor acts as the ultimate point of trust from which all subsequent verifications stem. Once a resolver has validated a signature chain from the root down to a specific domain, it can confidently assert that the DNS data it has received is authentic and has not been altered by a third party.

Public key cryptography is the enabler that makes DNSSEC a powerful tool against common DNS attacks. It prevents cache poisoning by ensuring that resolvers can detect forged or manipulated DNS responses. It safeguards against man-in-the-middle attacks by making it computationally infeasible for attackers to create valid signatures without the private key. By embedding trust directly into the DNS infrastructure, public key cryptography transforms DNS from a vulnerable, unauthenticated system into a secure and reliable framework for internet communication. This fundamental shift in the architecture of DNS helps protect users, businesses, and critical infrastructure from the growing array of cyber threats targeting the internet's core naming system.

Resource Record Types in DNSSEC

DNSSEC introduces several specialized resource record types that are essential for providing security to the traditional DNS system. These records extend the standard set of DNS resource records and are used to store cryptographic keys, digital signatures, and proof of non-existence. Each of these records plays a distinct role in creating the trust framework and cryptographic validation that defines DNSSEC.

Without them, the DNS would remain susceptible to tampering, spoofing, and cache poisoning attacks. Understanding these record types is crucial to comprehending how DNSSEC secures domain name resolution across the internet.

One of the most fundamental records introduced by DNSSEC is the DNSKEY record. The DNSKEY record stores the public keys that resolvers use to verify digital signatures. Every DNSSEC-signed zone contains at least one DNSKEY record, and in most cases, two distinct keys are used: the Key Signing Key (KSK) and the Zone Signing Key (ZSK). The KSK is used to sign the DNSKEY record set itself, while the ZSK is used to sign all other resource record sets within the zone. This separation of roles allows for more secure and manageable key rollover procedures. The DNSKEY record specifies the algorithm used, the key's cryptographic footprint, and the base64-encoded public key itself. Resolvers use the DNSKEY record to validate RRSIG records and thus confirm the authenticity and integrity of DNS data.

Closely tied to DNSKEY is the RRSIG record, which contains the digital signature for a particular resource record set (RRset). When a zone is signed with DNSSEC, each RRset is associated with an RRSIG record that holds the cryptographic signature created using the private key counterpart of the published DNSKEY. The RRSIG includes metadata such as the signature inception and expiration times, the signer's name, the algorithm used, and the signature itself. During DNS resolution, a validating resolver uses the corresponding DNSKEY to verify that the signature in the RRSIG record matches the queried DNS data. If the signature does not validate, the resolver will treat the DNS data as bogus and will not forward it to the client, thereby preventing the possibility of tampered responses being accepted.

Another essential record is the Delegation Signer or DS record, which is critical for establishing the chain of trust between a parent and a child zone. The DS record resides in the parent zone and contains a hash of the child zone's DNSKEY. It effectively links the child's zone key to the parent's trusted hierarchy. For example, the .com TLD will include DS records for second-level domains such as example.com. This link allows resolvers to continue validating signatures down the DNS hierarchy, starting from a trusted anchor such as the root zone's key. The DS record contains the key tag, the cryptographic algorithm used, the hash algorithm, and the actual hash of the child zone's public key. The proper configuration and publication of DS records are vital, as a missing or incorrect DS record will result in the breakdown of the chain of trust, leading to validation failures.

To handle situations where a query returns a negative response, DNSSEC uses NSEC and NSEC3 records. These records provide authenticated denial of existence, proving to resolvers that a particular domain name does not exist in a signed zone. In the case of an NSEC record, the server returns a record that lists the next existing domain name in the zone. By showing the gap between the queried name and the next valid name, the resolver can confirm that the requested name does not exist. However, this mechanism introduces a side effect called zone enumeration, where an attacker can potentially query sequential names and reconstruct a complete list of valid names in the zone.

To mitigate this risk, DNSSEC later introduced NSEC3 records. NSEC3 operates similarly to NSEC but uses a hashed version of the domain names instead of listing them in plain text. This hashing makes it more difficult for an attacker to enumerate all names within a zone, as the hashes are not easily reversible without significant computational effort. NSEC3 also includes optional parameters such as salt and iteration count, which further complicate efforts to precompute hashes and perform dictionary attacks on the hashed names. While not entirely immune to sophisticated attacks, NSEC3 greatly reduces the practicality of zone walking compared to plain NSEC.

Another less common but notable DNSSEC record type is NSEC3PARAM. This record is used to configure the parameters for NSEC3 within a zone. It specifies values such as the hash algorithm, salt, and iteration count that are applied during the generation of NSEC3 records. This record ensures consistency across the zone and allows resolvers to interpret NSEC3 hashes properly when verifying authenticated denial of existence.

Together, these records form the essential components of DNSSEC. The DNSKEY and DS records are crucial for building and maintaining the chain of trust across the DNS hierarchy. The RRSIG record ensures that data integrity is preserved, allowing resolvers to detect if any DNS data has been altered or forged. NSEC and NSEC3 provide the additional function of proving the non-existence of domains, protecting users and applications from forged NXDOMAIN responses that could otherwise redirect them to malicious sites.

Each time a resolver queries a DNSSEC-protected zone, it retrieves the relevant DNS records and their associated RRSIG signatures. The resolver then follows the chain of trust upward, checking the DS record in the parent zone and validating it against the DNSKEY record of the child zone. If everything checks out, the resolver knows the DNS data is authentic. If any part of the chain is broken, such as an invalid or missing signature, the resolver flags the data as bogus and blocks it from reaching the client.

The implementation of these DNSSEC-specific records requires zone administrators to carefully plan and maintain their DNS infrastructure. Keys must be securely generated and managed, signatures must be kept up to date to prevent them from expiring, and DS records must be correctly submitted to parent zones to maintain continuity of trust. Operational tasks such as key rollovers, NSEC3 parameter adjustments, and signature refreshes are all part of maintaining a healthy and secure DNSSEC-enabled zone.

Ultimately, these resource record types allow DNSSEC to fulfill its role in protecting the global DNS infrastructure. They introduce a layer of cryptographic certainty that traditional DNS lacks, making it vastly more difficult for attackers to manipulate DNS data undetected. By understanding how each record type contributes to the overall DNSSEC framework, administrators and security professionals can better secure their domains and contribute to a safer and more reliable internet.

DNSKEY and RRSIG Records

At the core of DNSSEC are two crucial record types: DNSKEY and RRSIG. These records work together to ensure the authenticity and integrity of DNS data, providing cryptographic assurance that a DNS response has not been altered in transit and originates from a legitimate source. Without DNSKEY and RRSIG records, the DNSSEC framework could not function, as these records form the basis of signature creation, signature validation, and ultimately the trust that resolvers place in the DNS data they receive.

The DNSKEY record stores the public key used in DNSSEC to verify digital signatures. Every DNSSEC-signed zone includes at least one DNSKEY record, though most zones will have multiple keys to serve different roles. The DNSKEY record is a critical element of the trust model in DNSSEC. It enables resolvers to validate the RRSIG signatures attached to DNS responses by using the public key contained in the DNSKEY record. The DNSKEY includes information such as the key's algorithm, the key's tag (a short numeric identifier), and the public key material itself, which is typically presented in base64-encoded form. This record type also specifies whether the key is a Zone Signing Key (ZSK) or a Key Signing Key (KSK), a distinction that is important for operational and security purposes.

The Zone Signing Key is used to sign the zone's data, including common DNS record types such as A, AAAA, MX, TXT, and others. These signatures are then stored in corresponding RRSIG records. The KSK, on the other hand, is used exclusively to sign the DNSKEY record set itself. This two-tiered approach to key usage allows for better key management, as the KSK, being more critical to the chain of trust with the parent zone, is rolled over less frequently and is usually stored with greater security. The separation between ZSK and KSK provides flexibility and minimizes operational risk. For example, if a ZSK is compromised, only the signatures of the zone data are affected. If a KSK is compromised, the chain of trust with the parent zone is at risk, requiring more extensive remediation.

The DNSKEY record is also tightly connected to the Delegation Signer (DS) record, which is placed in the parent zone to create a cryptographic link between the parent and child zones. When a zone administrator generates the KSK, a digest of the DNSKEY is created and published in the parent zone's DS record. This linkage allows resolvers to validate the DNSKEY using information from the parent zone, thereby extending the chain of trust from the root zone all the way down to the authoritative zone being queried.

Complementing the DNSKEY is the RRSIG record, which holds the digital signature for each resource record set (RRset) in the signed zone. The RRSIG record is generated by applying the private key corresponding to the DNSKEY to a cryptographic hash of the RRset. The resulting digital signature is then attached to the DNS data as an RRSIG record. The RRSIG contains metadata such as the type of data it covers (for example, A records or MX records), the algorithm used for the signature, the signature's validity period (inception and expiration times), and the signer's domain name. The actual digital signature is included as a base64-encoded string.

When a resolver queries a DNSSEC-enabled zone, it receives both the DNS data (such as an A record for a hostname) and the corresponding RRSIG. The resolver retrieves the DNSKEY record for the zone and uses the public key within that record to verify the signature in the RRSIG. If the signature checks out, the resolver knows that the DNS data is authentic and has not been tampered with since it was signed. If the signature fails to validate or is missing entirely when it is expected, the resolver will flag the response as bogus and will not forward the data to the client.

The combination of DNSKEY and RRSIG ensures data integrity in DNS transactions. Any modification to DNS records after they have been signed, whether by a malicious actor or accidental corruption, will result in a signature mismatch during validation. This capability is what allows DNSSEC to thwart cache poisoning and other tampering attacks. Even if an attacker successfully intercepts and alters a DNS response, they cannot forge a valid signature without access to the private key used to generate the RRSIG record.

Operationally, the DNSKEY and RRSIG records also bring about additional considerations. Because RRSIG records include an expiration date, zones must be regularly re-signed to ensure that the signatures remain valid. This process is typically automated to prevent service disruptions caused by expired signatures. Similarly, key rollovers for both ZSK and KSK must be planned and executed carefully. A ZSK rollover involves generating a new key pair and re-signing the zone, while a KSK rollover also requires updating the DS record in the parent zone to reflect the new key's digest.

DNSKEY and RRSIG records also increase the size of DNS responses. Each signed RRset generates its own RRSIG record, and the DNSKEY record set itself may include multiple keys, particularly in environments that support algorithm rollover or multi-algorithm signing for compatibility reasons. These larger DNS responses can exceed the traditional 512-byte limit for UDP packets, requiring the use of EDNS0 extensions and sometimes fallback to TCP to accommodate the additional data.

In terms of cryptographic algorithms, DNSKEY records can specify a variety of algorithms approved for use with DNSSEC, including RSA/SHA-256, RSA/SHA-512, and elliptic curve options like ECDSA P-256. The choice of algorithm affects the size of the DNSKEY and RRSIG records as well as the computational overhead on both the authoritative server performing the signing and the resolver validating the signature. Elliptic curve algorithms are particularly appealing for their smaller key sizes and faster processing times while maintaining strong security guarantees.

The DNSKEY and RRSIG records work together to form the foundation of DNSSEC's security model. By leveraging public key cryptography, these records ensure that DNS data can be verified by resolvers worldwide, providing confidence that the answers returned by DNS servers are legitimate and have not been manipulated. Their proper implementation and management are essential to maintaining the integrity and reliability of DNSSEC-protected zones. As DNSSEC adoption continues to grow, DNSKEY and RRSIG records will remain vital elements in safeguarding the DNS infrastructure that underpins the modern internet.

NSEC and NSEC3 Records

Within the DNSSEC framework, NSEC and NSEC3 records serve a critical role by providing authenticated denial of existence. When a resolver queries for a domain name or record type that does not exist, the DNS server must not only return a negative response but also prove that the non-existence of that data is legitimate and verifiable. Without this feature, attackers could attempt to forge NXDOMAIN responses or manipulate DNS replies to mislead users or redirect traffic. NSEC and NSEC3 records solve this problem by cryptographically signing negative responses, allowing resolvers to confirm that a queried domain or record truly does not exist within the DNS zone.

The NSEC record, short for Next Secure record, was the first mechanism introduced by DNSSEC to enable authenticated denial of existence. When a resolver queries for a non-existent name, the authoritative DNS server responds with an NSEC record indicating the two closest valid domain names in lexicographical order within the zone. This record shows that there are no valid names between these two points, and therefore the queried name does not exist. For example, if a resolver queries for nonexistent.example.com, the server might return an NSEC record showing that alpha.example.com comes before nonexistent.example.com, and omega.example.com comes after. This confirms that nonexistent.example.com is not present between those two valid names.

The NSEC record also includes a type bitmap, which lists all the valid record types available for the domain preceding the next domain in the sequence. This feature allows resolvers to also authenticate negative responses for missing record types. For instance, if a resolver queries for an MX record for a domain but only A and AAAA records exist, the NSEC record will confirm the absence of an MX record in a verifiable way. This mechanism protects against certain attacks that might attempt to forge missing records to redirect or block legitimate traffic.

However, the design of NSEC introduced an unintended side effect known as zone walking or zone enumeration. Because NSEC records reveal the next valid domain name in lexicographical order, an attacker can query systematically through the zone and piece together a full list of valid domain names. While this might not seem like a severe security flaw in all contexts, in environments where the naming of internal services or private infrastructure could reveal sensitive information, zone enumeration can become a significant concern. Attackers could use the discovered names to map networks, identify internal systems, or launch targeted attacks against specific hosts.

To address this issue, the NSEC3 record was introduced as an enhancement to provide the same authenticated denial of existence functionality while reducing the risk of zone walking. NSEC3 modifies the process by returning hashes of domain names instead of cleartext names. When a resolver queries for a non-existent domain, the NSEC3 record will provide hashes of the next valid names in the hash ordering, along with the type bitmap as in NSEC. Since the hashes are computationally difficult to reverse without knowing the original domain names, this approach mitigates the ability of an attacker to easily enumerate the zone.

The NSEC3 record includes several parameters that control its behavior. One important element is the hash algorithm used, which is typically SHA-1 as specified by the DNSSEC standards. In addition, the NSEC3 record contains a salt value and an iteration count. The salt is a random value that is appended to each domain name before hashing, making precomputed hash tables less effective. The iteration count defines how many times the hashing algorithm is applied, increasing the computational work required to brute-force or reverse-engineer the hashes. By tuning these parameters, zone administrators can strike a balance between security and performance, as higher iteration counts provide stronger resistance to attacks but require more processing power from both the server and resolver.

While NSEC3 mitigates zone enumeration, it does not eliminate it entirely. A determined attacker with sufficient resources may still attempt to brute-force hashes, especially for zones with predictable or simple domain names. Nevertheless, NSEC3 significantly raises the barrier to such attacks compared to plain NSEC, making it the preferred choice for many organizations concerned about zone confidentiality.

Another variation of NSEC3 is the concept of Opt-Out, which is particularly useful for large zones that delegate many unsigned subdomains. In such cases, NSEC3 Opt-Out allows DNS administrators to exclude unsigned delegations from the hashed range covered by an NSEC3 record. This reduces the size of the NSEC3 chain and the number of records that need to be signed, improving efficiency while maintaining DNSSEC protection for signed portions of the zone. However, Opt-Out must be carefully configured, as it introduces trade-offs in terms of validation completeness.

Operationally, the deployment of NSEC or NSEC3 records requires that zones be fully signed and that every non-existent name within the zone can be proved as such using these records. When a resolver queries a signed zone and receives a negative response, the resolver retrieves and validates the NSEC or NSEC3 record along with its RRSIG signature. The resolver checks the digital signature using the corresponding DNSKEY record to ensure that the denial is authentic and has not been forged or manipulated in transit. If the validation fails, the resolver considers the negative response invalid and treats the data as bogus, protecting users from potential forgery.

The use of NSEC and NSEC3 records underscores the importance of comprehensive security in DNSSEC. Securing only positive responses would leave negative answers vulnerable to exploitation. By cryptographically proving the absence of data, these records complete the trust model that DNSSEC introduces to the DNS infrastructure. They prevent attackers from crafting fraudulent NXDOMAIN responses or falsely claiming that legitimate data does not exist.

NSEC and NSEC3 records are essential tools for DNS administrators who wish to deploy DNSSEC effectively. They not only ensure that all DNS responses, whether positive or negative, are trustworthy but also provide configurable mechanisms to address concerns about zone enumeration. As more organizations and service providers adopt DNSSEC to protect their domains, the proper implementation and management of NSEC and NSEC3 records will remain fundamental to maintaining a secure, resilient, and trustworthy DNS ecosystem.

DS Records and Delegation Signer Chains

The Delegation Signer (DS) record is one of the most crucial components in the DNSSEC trust model, serving as the essential link that connects a parent zone to a child zone in the DNS hierarchy. DS records establish and extend the chain of trust, allowing DNS resolvers to verify that a particular zone's public key is authentic and authorized by its parent zone. Without the DS record, DNSSEC's ability to provide end-to-end validation from the root of the DNS down to individual domain names would not be possible. The DS record is a fundamental part of DNSSEC's design and is vital to the propagation of trust across different levels of the domain name system.

When a zone administrator signs a DNS zone using DNSSEC, the process begins with the generation of a pair of cryptographic keys. The public key is published in the zone's DNSKEY record, while the private key is kept secret and is used to sign the zone's records. To link this signed zone to its parent zone, a hash of the DNSKEY record is created and placed in the parent zone as a DS record. This DS record acts as a fingerprint of the child zone's DNSKEY, allowing resolvers to verify that the child's key has been vouched for by the parent.

A DS record contains several fields, each of which plays an important role in its operation. It includes the key tag, which is a short numeric identifier derived from the DNSKEY record; the algorithm number, which specifies the cryptographic algorithm used to generate the key; the digest type, which indicates the hashing algorithm applied to the DNSKEY; and finally, the digest itself, which is the hash of the DNSKEY. This digest is the critical element that ties the DS record to the child zone's DNSKEY record. During the DNSSEC validation process, a resolver uses the DS record to validate the authenticity of the child zone's public key, ensuring that the DNSKEY presented by the child zone matches the digest published by the parent.

The chain of trust begins at the root zone, which is considered the ultimate trust anchor and is widely configured in validating resolvers. The root zone contains DS records for all the top-level domains (TLDs), such as .com, .org, and country-code TLDs like .uk or .jp. These TLDs, in turn, contain DS records for second-level domains, such as example.com or university.edu. This delegation process continues down the hierarchy, with each level providing cryptographic proof that the next level's public key is legitimate. The resolver follows this path from the root trust anchor down to the target domain, validating each DS and DNSKEY record pair along the way.

The integrity of the DS record is guaranteed by the fact that it resides in the parent zone, which itself is signed by the parent's private key. The DS record is also accompanied by an RRSIG record, as is standard with DNSSEC-protected data. This allows resolvers to verify the DS record using the DNSKEY of the parent zone. If this verification is successful, the resolver proceeds to retrieve the child zone's DNSKEY and validate that it matches the hash contained in the DS record. If the DS record is missing or the DNSKEY fails to match the DS digest, the resolver will consider the chain of trust broken, and the DNS response will be treated as untrustworthy.

The delegation signer chain that results from the propagation of DS records from the root down to individual zones is the backbone of DNSSEC validation. Each link in this chain reinforces the assurance that the DNS data being retrieved is authoritative and has not been tampered with. For example, if a resolver queries for www.example.com, and example.com is a signed zone with a valid DS record in the .com TLD, the resolver can validate the DNSKEY for example.com by verifying the DS record within the .com zone. This process continues up to the root, where the resolver ultimately verifies the root's key using its pre-configured trust anchor.

Maintaining a proper DS record is essential for DNSSEC-enabled zones. If a DS record is incorrectly configured, it can cause validation failures and prevent users from resolving the affected domain. One common operational challenge arises during key rollovers, particularly when the Key Signing Key (KSK) is changed. Since the DS record contains a hash of the KSK, any KSK rollover requires the creation of a new DS record and its timely submission to the parent zone. Failure to update the DS record in the parent zone after a KSK rollover will result in a mismatch between the parent's DS record and the child's new DNSKEY, effectively breaking the chain of trust and rendering the zone unresolvable to validating resolvers.

Another key aspect of DS records is their role in enabling selective signing strategies and policy enforcement. Organizations can choose whether or not to sign specific subzones, and the presence or absence of DS records in the parent zone reflects these decisions. If a subzone is delegated but lacks a corresponding DS record in the parent, resolvers understand that DNSSEC validation does not apply to that subzone, and standard DNS resolution will proceed without signature verification. This flexibility allows administrators to control the scope of DNSSEC deployment within large and complex DNS infrastructures.

DS records also facilitate trust in delegation scenarios where an organization operates multiple zones or subdomains. By carefully managing DS records, administrators can ensure that secure delegations extend across the entirety of their namespace, reinforcing security while enabling scalability and modular management of DNSSEC across their domain structure.

The deployment and maintenance of DS records require coordination between the child zone administrator and the parent zone operator, such as a TLD registry or registrar. Many registries now support automated mechanisms, including EPP (Extensible Provisioning Protocol) extensions, that allow registrars to submit DS records more efficiently on behalf of their customers. Despite this automation, care must still be taken to verify the correctness of DS record data, especially during key rollovers, domain transfers, or registrar changes.

The DS record and the delegation signer chain that it enables are vital pillars of the DNSSEC architecture. They extend cryptographic trust from one zone to the next, providing a continuous and verifiable path from the root of the DNS down to individual resource records. This structure transforms DNS into a secure and reliable naming service, ensuring that resolvers and, ultimately, end users can trust that the information they receive is genuine and has not been compromised. By maintaining accurate and properly signed DS records, organizations contribute to the broader health and security of the global DNS ecosystem.

Zone Signing Explained

Zone signing is one of the most critical steps in implementing DNSSEC, as it is the process by which DNS data within a zone is cryptographically secured. The goal of zone signing is to ensure that every record set (RRset) in the DNS zone file is digitally signed, allowing resolvers to verify the authenticity and integrity of the DNS data they receive. Without zone signing, DNSSEC would not be able to provide protection against common threats such as cache poisoning, man-in-the-middle attacks, or data tampering during DNS resolution.

Understanding how zone signing works, from key generation to signature creation, is essential for any organization deploying DNSSEC.

The process of zone signing begins with the generation of cryptographic key pairs. In a typical DNSSEC deployment, two pairs of keys are created: the Zone Signing Key (ZSK) and the Key Signing Key (KSK). Both are asymmetric cryptographic keys, consisting of a private key used for signing and a public key that is distributed within the zone's DNSKEY records. The KSK is primarily responsible for signing the DNSKEY record set, while the ZSK signs all other RRsets in the zone. This separation allows for better security and operational flexibility because the KSK is rolled over less frequently, whereas the ZSK is updated more regularly to limit potential exposure.

Once the keys have been generated, the next step is to apply digital signatures to the RRsets within the zone. An RRset is a collection of DNS resource records with the same name, class, and type. For example, all A records associated with www.example.com form a single RRset. The private ZSK is used to create a cryptographic hash of each RRset, which is then signed to produce a digital signature. This signature is stored in a new DNSSEC-specific record called an RRSIG record, which is placed in the zone alongside the corresponding RRset.

For the DNSKEY record set itself, the private KSK is used to create its signature, resulting in an RRSIG record that covers the DNSKEY records. This is crucial because the DNSKEY record set includes the public keys necessary for resolvers to validate all other signatures in the zone. The signed DNSKEY RRset forms the starting point for validation within the zone and must link to the parent zone via the DS record published by the parent.

Once all relevant RRsets have been signed, the signed zone is ready to be published to authoritative DNS servers. At this point, when a resolver queries the zone, the authoritative server will respond not only with the requested DNS records but also with the corresponding RRSIG records. This allows the resolver to use the public key found in the DNSKEY record to verify the signatures, ensuring that the data has not been tampered with and is authentic.

Zone signing is not a one-time operation. DNS data frequently changes due to updates such as new subdomains being created, IP address changes, or new records being added to the zone. Each time an RRset is modified, it must be re-signed with the ZSK to generate a fresh RRSIG record. Additionally, every signature has an inception and expiration date, meaning signatures must be periodically regenerated even if the underlying DNS data remains the same. This prevents old signatures from being reused in potential replay attacks and ensures that only current, valid signatures are used during resolution.

Automating the zone signing process is a best practice, especially for large and dynamic zones. Most modern DNS software supports automatic signing, where the signing process is integrated into the DNS server's operation, automatically generating new RRSIG records as necessary. This reduces the risk of human error and ensures that signatures remain valid and up to date. Automated systems can also handle key rollovers, re-signing the entire zone when a new ZSK or KSK is introduced.

Zone signing also requires careful consideration of performance and efficiency. Each signed RRset and corresponding RRSIG increases the size of DNS responses. While the DNS protocol supports large responses through EDNS0 and TCP fallback mechanisms, administrators must ensure that their infrastructure can handle the increased traffic and that firewalls and network devices allow larger DNS packets. Improperly sized responses may be truncated, leading to resolution failures or degraded performance for end users.

In terms of security, protecting the private ZSK and KSK is paramount. If an attacker gains access to these keys, they could forge valid signatures and manipulate DNS data undetected. Private keys should be stored securely, often within Hardware Security Modules (HSMs) or other secure environments with strict access controls. Regular audits of key management practices, secure key storage, and strict access policies help prevent unauthorized access and maintain the integrity of zone signing operations.

Another operational consideration in zone signing is the management of rollover events. ZSK rollovers are relatively common and should be performed regularly as part of standard security hygiene. During a ZSK rollover, the old and new ZSKs may coexist temporarily in the DNSKEY RRset to ensure continuity of validation for resolvers that may still have cached signatures from the old key. KSK rollovers are less frequent but more impactful because they require updating the DS record in the parent zone to reflect the hash of the new KSK. Improper management of KSK rollovers can break the chain of trust and result in DNS resolution failures for the affected domain.

Zone signing with DNSSEC also improves resilience against certain types of attacks. For example, signed zones cannot be easily poisoned by cache injection attacks, as resolvers will reject any forged data that lacks valid signatures. Similarly, man-in-the-middle attackers cannot alter DNS responses or redirect users to malicious destinations without detection, as they cannot forge RRSIG records without access to the private signing keys.

Overall, zone signing is the operational core of DNSSEC. It transforms a traditional DNS zone file into a cryptographically secure zone that can defend itself against a wide range of attacks. By applying digital signatures to every RRset, the zone guarantees that its data is authentic, untampered, and verifiable by anyone querying the DNS. Properly executed zone signing strengthens the security and reliability of internet communications, protecting users and organizations alike from a variety of DNS-based threats.

The DNSSEC Trust Anchor

The DNSSEC trust anchor is the foundational element that makes the entire DNSSEC validation process possible. It serves as the starting point of the chain of trust that DNSSEC establishes throughout the DNS hierarchy. In cryptographic systems, a trust anchor is a known, trusted public key or set of keys that is assumed to be correct and is used as the base for validating digital signatures. In DNSSEC, this trust anchor is typically the public key for the DNS root zone's Key Signing Key (KSK). Without a trust anchor, a validating resolver would have no initial point of trust from which to begin verifying DNSSEC-protected data.

In the DNSSEC model, each level of the DNS hierarchy—from the root zone to top-level domains, second-level domains, and subdomains—signs its records and establishes a chain of trust through Delegation Signer (DS) records linking parent and child zones. However, for this chain of trust to be meaningful, there must be a universally accepted root from which validation can begin. The DNS root zone serves this purpose. The public key associated with the root zone's KSK is widely distributed and configured in DNS resolvers around the world. This key is hard-coded or configured manually as the trust anchor in the resolver's settings. When a resolver receives a DNS response from any domain, it validates the chain of trust by working upward from the domain to the root, confirming signatures at each step using the DS and DNSKEY records. The trust anchor is where this verification process culminates, providing confidence that the entire chain below it is trustworthy.

The DNS root zone was first signed with DNSSEC in 2010, an event often referred to as the DNSSEC root signing ceremony. This was a pivotal milestone in global internet security. Prior to this event, DNSSEC could only be partially deployed, and validators had to rely on manually configured trust anchors for individual zones. The signing of the root allowed for the full hierarchical model of DNSSEC to be realized, enabling automated trust chains from the root down to any signed domain. Today, the root trust anchor is embedded by default in most modern validating resolvers, including widely used software such as BIND, Unbound, and PowerDNS.

The trust anchor is critical because it is the only part of the DNSSEC trust model that is not validated through DNSSEC itself. Instead, it is trusted implicitly. Every other DNSKEY and DS record pair in the DNS hierarchy is validated by the resolver through cryptographic means, but the root KSK is trusted as the initial step in the process. This makes the secure distribution and management of the trust anchor key a matter of significant importance. To address this, the Internet Assigned Numbers Authority (IANA) and the Internet Corporation for Assigned Names and Numbers (ICANN) jointly oversee a highly formalized and secure process for managing the root KSK. This process includes the highly publicized key signing ceremonies where the root key is used to sign the root zone's DNSKEY RRset.

The trust anchor also plays a crucial role in resolver behavior when validating DNSSEC responses. When a resolver queries a signed domain, it checks the chain of trust from the queried domain up to the root. If the resolver cannot establish a valid chain of trust that terminates at the configured trust anchor, it will treat the DNS data as bogus and will not return it to the client. This security mechanism ensures that DNS responses without a complete and valid trust path are rejected, protecting users from tampered or forged DNS data. However, it also means that if the trust anchor is outdated or incorrectly configured, the resolver will fail to validate even legitimate DNS responses, potentially causing service disruptions.

To avoid such issues, IANA provides a mechanism for automated trust anchor management through RFC 5011. This standard allows DNS resolvers to automatically update their trust anchors over time by monitoring DNSKEY records in the root zone for indications that a new KSK has been introduced and signed by the old KSK. This key rollover mechanism ensures that resolvers stay in sync with changes to the trust anchor without requiring manual intervention from system administrators. Nonetheless, many organizations, particularly those with critical infrastructure, still choose to manually manage their trust anchors to retain full control over the process.

The security of the trust anchor is paramount because any compromise of the root KSK would undermine the integrity of the entire DNSSEC-protected DNS. If an attacker gained control over the root private key, they could theoretically sign false data for any domain on the internet, breaking the very trust that DNSSEC is designed to create. This is why the operational procedures for generating, storing, and using the root KSK are subject to rigorous security controls, including secure facilities, hardware security modules, multi-party control, and comprehensive auditing.

Another important function of the trust anchor is its role in global interoperability. By having a single, universally trusted key for the root zone, DNSSEC allows any resolver in the world to validate DNS responses consistently and securely. Whether a user is in North America, Europe, Asia, or any other region, the trust anchor provides a common point of reference that enables secure name resolution on a global scale. This shared trust model is one of the key reasons DNSSEC has been successful in improving the security of DNS infrastructure worldwide.

In addition to the root zone trust anchor, there are scenarios where administrators may configure additional trust anchors. For instance, in environments where internal zones are signed with DNSSEC but do not have a complete chain of trust to the root, administrators might manually configure trust anchors for these internal zones. This is common in private networks or isolated environments, such as corporate intranets, where DNSSEC is used to secure internal naming structures without relying on public TLDs.

Despite its importance, the trust anchor is often an invisible component for end users and even for many system operators. Its role is typically automated and integrated into resolver software, functioning silently in the background to validate DNSSEC signatures. However, behind this apparent simplicity lies a highly sophisticated and critical piece of global internet infrastructure. The DNSSEC trust anchor enables billions of secure DNS queries every day, providing the assurance that internet users are reaching authentic, untampered destinations. This foundational element remains one of the key pillars supporting trust and security across the modern internet.

DNSSEC Chain of Trust

The DNSSEC chain of trust is the structural backbone of how Domain Name System Security Extensions provide security and ensure data authenticity across the global DNS infrastructure. It is a hierarchical, cryptographically verifiable model that links each DNS zone to its parent zone, all the way up to the root zone. This model allows recursive resolvers to validate DNS responses by verifying each step in the DNS hierarchy, ensuring that the information they receive has not been altered, forged, or tampered with. Without the chain of trust, DNSSEC would not be able to offer the assurance and protection that organizations and users depend on to mitigate the risks inherent in DNS queries.

The chain of trust starts with the root zone, which serves as the ultimate trust anchor. The root zone is signed with a Key Signing Key (KSK), and this key is pre-configured in most validating resolvers as the default trust anchor. The root zone contains Delegation Signer (DS) records for every signed top-level domain (TLD), such as .com, .org, .net, or country-code TLDs like .uk and .de. These DS records link the root zone to the public keys of each TLD by containing a hash of the TLD's DNSKEY record. When a resolver queries a domain under a TLD, such as example.com, it will look for the DS record in the .com zone and validate it using the root's DNSKEY. Once the DS record has been validated, the resolver retrieves the DNSKEY from the example.com zone and verifies that it matches the DS record, continuing the chain.

This process repeats down the DNS hierarchy. The example.com zone may delegate to subdomains such as mail.example.com or app.example.com, and if these subdomains are independently signed, they will have their own DNSKEY records and corresponding DS records in the example.com parent zone. Each link between parent and child zones is established through a DS and DNSKEY pair, creating a seamless cryptographic path from the root down to the queried domain. The resolver validates this chain step by step, confirming that every zone involved has properly signed its records and that each level has authorized the next level below.

Each zone in the DNS hierarchy that participates in DNSSEC signing plays a dual role. It serves as a child zone, responsible for publishing a DNSKEY record that is linked to the DS record in its parent, and it acts as a parent zone, publishing DS records for any signed subdomains that it delegates. This structure allows for a distributed trust model where responsibility is shared between numerous independent entities. The root zone is managed by IANA and ICANN, the TLD zones by various registries, and second-level and lower domains by registrars, companies, and organizations around the world. Despite this decentralization, the DNSSEC chain of trust connects them into a single verifiable system.

Resolvers rely heavily on this chain of trust when performing DNSSEC validation. For instance, when a resolver queries for www.example.com, it will follow the entire chain from the root trust anchor. First, it checks the DS record for .com in the root zone and verifies the associated DNSKEY. Next, it queries the .com zone and validates the DS record for example.com. Finally, it queries example.com and retrieves the DNSKEY used to validate the signed DNS data. If any part of this chain is missing or invalid—for example, if the DS record is absent, the signature is incorrect, or a key does not match its parent's DS record—the resolver will consider the entire validation process a failure, marking the response as bogus and preventing potentially forged data from being passed on to the end user.

One of the strengths of the DNSSEC chain of trust is that it creates a self-healing and globally distributed system for data authentication. Even if a domain is served from multiple authoritative servers in different parts of the world, resolvers everywhere can independently validate the authenticity of the DNS responses they receive. This greatly reduces the risk of successful cache poisoning attacks, as an attacker would not only need to forge DNS data but also generate valid signatures backed by private keys that they do not possess.

Another advantage of the chain of trust is its resilience and scalability. DNSSEC's design mirrors the structure of the DNS itself, which is built to scale to billions of domains across the globe. Every new domain added to the DNS can be integrated into the chain of trust by signing the zone and ensuring that its parent zone correctly publishes its DS record. This allows the security provided by DNSSEC to extend naturally alongside the growth of the internet, without needing centralized control or limiting how DNS operates.

However, maintaining the chain of trust requires strict operational discipline. Key Signing Key rollovers, DNSKEY record changes, and the publication of DS records in parent zones must be meticulously coordinated. If a zone's KSK is replaced but the DS record in the parent is not updated to reflect the new key, resolvers will be unable to validate the chain, leading to service disruptions. Similarly, errors in signing, such as missing RRSIG records or improperly configured DNSKEY records, can cause validation failures and undermine the availability of DNS services for the affected domain.

The robustness of the chain of trust also depends on the security of the private keys used in signing operations. The compromise of a private key anywhere in the chain could allow an attacker to forge valid signatures and impersonate the signed zone. This is why best practices recommend secure storage of private keys, frequent ZSK rollovers, and tightly controlled KSK rollover procedures. Many organizations use hardware security modules (HSMs) to generate and protect their DNSSEC private keys, ensuring that signing operations occur within secure environments.

The DNSSEC chain of trust has become a critical component of modern internet infrastructure. It strengthens the integrity of DNS, prevents tampering, and builds confidence among users and organizations that the DNS data they rely on is legitimate. As DNSSEC adoption has grown, with most major TLDs and many second-level domains participating, the chain of trust has expanded to secure a significant portion of global DNS traffic.

The DNSSEC chain of trust creates a layered defense system that secures DNS queries by design. From the root zone down to the individual domain level, this chain ensures that resolvers can independently verify the authenticity of DNS data and protect users from a variety of threats. Its hierarchical nature, coupled with the decentralized administration of the DNS, allows for a globally distributed and highly resilient security model that helps to safeguard one of the internet's most vital protocols.

DNSSEC Validation Process

The DNSSEC validation process is the mechanism by which DNS resolvers verify the authenticity and integrity of DNS data received from authoritative servers. This process ensures that the information returned in response to a query has not been tampered with, forged, or altered by any intermediary. Unlike traditional DNS, which operates without security checks and accepts data as-is, DNSSEC introduces a set of cryptographic validations that resolvers perform on every signed response. This validation process is critical to maintaining the chain of trust that DNSSEC establishes from the root zone to the queried domain.

When a client, such as a web browser or an application, requests the IP address for a domain name, it initiates a DNS query that is typically handled by a recursive resolver. If the resolver is DNSSEC-aware and configured to validate signatures, it begins by checking whether the domain in question is DNSSEC-signed. If the domain is not signed, the resolver will proceed as it would under traditional DNS, simply returning the data to the client. However, if the domain is part of a signed zone, the resolver initiates the DNSSEC validation process.

The first step in the validation process is to examine the DNS response received from the authoritative server. Alongside the requested data, such as an A or AAAA record, the authoritative server also includes an RRSIG record. This RRSIG record contains a digital signature that corresponds to the resource record set (RRset) returned in the answer section of the DNS response. The resolver extracts this RRSIG and identifies which DNSKEY record is needed to verify it. The DNSKEY record resides in the DNSKEY RRset within the same zone.

To validate the signature, the resolver queries for the DNSKEY record associated with the zone. Once obtained, it uses the public key contained within the DNSKEY record to cryptographically verify the RRSIG signature over the RRset. If the signature is valid, the resolver can confirm that the DNS data has not been altered since it was signed by the authoritative server's private key. If the signature fails validation, the resolver treats the data as bogus and refuses to forward it to the client.

The validation process does not stop with the verification of the DNSKEY and RRSIG pair. The resolver must also verify that the DNSKEY record itself is authentic. This is where the chain of trust becomes essential. The resolver checks for the Delegation Signer (DS) record in the parent zone, which contains a hash of the child zone's DNSKEY. The DS record is signed with the parent zone's private key and comes with its own RRSIG. The resolver then queries the parent zone for the DS record and its corresponding RRSIG, validating the signature using the parent zone's DNSKEY.

This hierarchical validation continues upwards, from the child zone to its parent zone, then to the grandparent zone, until the resolver eventually reaches the root zone. The root zone, signed with its own

KSK, serves as the trust anchor, and its DNSKEY is pre-configured in the resolver's trusted key store. The root DNSKEY is considered inherently trustworthy, and it is used to validate the RRSIG for the DS record of the top-level domain, such as .com or .org.

Throughout this process, the resolver follows strict validation logic. If all the signatures validate correctly from the domain being queried all the way up to the root trust anchor, the DNS data is marked as secure, and the resolver passes it to the client. If at any point a signature cannot be validated, a key does not match its corresponding DS record, or if a necessary DNSSEC record is missing, the resolver flags the data as bogus. Bogus responses are not delivered to the client, effectively blocking forged or malicious data from propagating further.

Another important aspect of the DNSSEC validation process is authenticated denial of existence. When a resolver queries for a domain or record that does not exist, the authoritative server returns either an NSEC or NSEC3 record, along with an RRSIG. These records prove that no such domain or record is present in the zone. The resolver validates the RRSIG associated with the NSEC or NSEC3 record, confirming that the non-existence response is legitimate and not forged by an attacker attempting to block access to valid domains or divert traffic.

Resolvers also cache DNSSEC validation results for efficiency. Once a resolver successfully validates a DNSKEY, DS, or RRSIG record, it stores the result in its cache until the record's time-to-live (TTL) expires. This allows subsequent queries to be resolved more quickly without repeating the entire validation process, provided that the cached records are still valid and unexpired.

Resolvers must also handle key rollovers as part of the validation process. When a zone administrator rolls over the Zone Signing Key or the Key Signing Key, the DNSKEY RRset will include both the old and new keys temporarily. During this period, resolvers can validate signatures using either key to ensure uninterrupted service. After the rollover completes and the old key is removed, resolvers rely solely on the new key and its associated DS record from the parent zone.

The DNSSEC validation process adds additional processing overhead for recursive resolvers, as cryptographic signature checks must be performed and multiple queries may be needed to complete the chain of trust. However, modern resolvers and hardware are optimized to handle this load efficiently, and the security benefits outweigh the added complexity. The assurance that DNS data is verified at every level of the hierarchy provides strong protection against common attacks such as DNS spoofing and cache poisoning.

In environments where DNSSEC validation is widely implemented, users benefit from enhanced trust in the responses they receive from DNS. Financial institutions, government services, and security-sensitive applications increasingly depend on DNSSEC validation to ensure that users are connecting to legitimate, authorized servers. DNSSEC validation is especially valuable in mitigating sophisticated cyber attacks where adversaries may seek to redirect users to malicious sites or interfere with DNS resolution to disrupt services.

Ultimately, DNSSEC validation is the engine that enforces the security guarantees provided by DNSSEC. By meticulously verifying signatures at every step of the DNS hierarchy, resolvers create a secure and tamper-evident system that defends the integrity of one of the internet's most foundational protocols. As more organizations and users rely on DNSSEC-enabled resolvers, the global DNS ecosystem becomes more resilient to a wide range of threats.

Implementing DNSSEC in Small Networks

Implementing DNSSEC in small networks presents unique opportunities and challenges. While large enterprises and global service providers may have dedicated teams and resources for securing DNS infrastructure, small businesses, educational institutions, and local organizations often have limited budgets and personnel to manage such implementations. However, these smaller environments still rely on DNS as a critical service and are equally vulnerable to threats like cache poisoning, DNS spoofing, and man-in-the-middle attacks. Deploying DNSSEC in these settings not only enhances security but also demonstrates a proactive commitment to protecting internal resources, employees, and users from external threats.

The first step in implementing DNSSEC in a small network is to assess the current DNS environment. Many small networks either outsource their DNS hosting to a third-party provider or run a local DNS server using software such as BIND, Unbound, or PowerDNS. If DNS is outsourced to a domain registrar or DNS hosting company, the implementation process may simply involve enabling DNSSEC through the provider's management portal. Most modern DNS hosting platforms support DNSSEC signing as a service, automatically generating DNSKEY and RRSIG records, handling key rollovers, and managing Delegation Signer (DS) records with the parent zone. In this scenario, administrators only need to activate DNSSEC and confirm that the registrar submits the correct DS record to the top-level domain registry.

For small networks managing their own authoritative DNS servers, implementing DNSSEC involves additional technical steps. The process starts with generating the cryptographic keys required for signing the zone. Typically, administrators will create both a Zone Signing Key (ZSK) and a Key Signing Key (KSK). The private components of these keys are used to sign DNS records within the zone, while the public keys are published in DNSKEY records. The signed zone must then be configured to include RRSIG records for every resource record set, as well as NSEC or NSEC3 records for authenticated denial of existence. Tools such as BIND's dnssec-keygen and dnssec-signzone can automate much of this process, helping small teams with limited experience in cryptographic operations.

Once the zone is signed, the next crucial task is submitting the DS record to the parent zone. This step links the signed zone to the broader DNSSEC trust chain and enables resolvers to validate responses originating from the small network's domain. Without the DS record in place at the registrar level, external resolvers cannot complete the chain of trust, rendering the DNSSEC implementation ineffective from the perspective of outside users. Small network administrators must ensure that the DS record is properly submitted and verified, typically through their domain registrar's control panel or customer support channels.

In addition to securing the authoritative DNS infrastructure, small networks may also wish to deploy validating resolvers for their internal users. Running a local DNS resolver with DNSSEC validation capabilities ensures that all outbound DNS queries from the network are subject to signature verification, blocking any forged or tampered responses originating from external threats. Software such as Unbound or BIND can be configured to act as recursive resolvers with DNSSEC validation enabled by default. By installing and configuring a local validating resolver, administrators can add a layer of protection for users within the network without depending solely on external resolver services.

While the technical process of implementing DNSSEC in a small network is well-documented and supported by modern DNS software, operational considerations must also be addressed. DNSSEC introduces additional complexity compared to traditional DNS, and small teams need to plan for routine maintenance tasks such as key rollovers, signature expiration monitoring, and troubleshooting validation failures. Automating key management using tools like BIND's inline-signing feature or OpenDNSSEC can simplify these tasks by automatically re-signing zones and handling ZSK rollovers without manual intervention. However, the KSK rollover process still requires coordination with the parent zone to update the DS record, which must be handled carefully to prevent trust chain disruptions.

Another factor to consider is the increased size of DNS responses due to the inclusion of RRSIG and DNSKEY records. Small networks should ensure that their infrastructure supports Extension Mechanisms for DNS (EDNS0) and can handle DNS messages larger than 512 bytes. Firewalls, routers, and network security devices must be configured to allow larger UDP packets or to properly support TCP fallback for DNS traffic when necessary. Failure to accommodate the larger DNSSEC payloads can result in truncated responses and resolution failures, leading to user frustration and potential downtime.

Despite these complexities, DNSSEC implementation in small networks brings significant benefits. It prevents external attackers from injecting malicious data into the DNS resolution process, protects internal services from redirection attacks, and enhances the overall security posture of the organization. For environments such as healthcare providers, legal offices, educational institutions, or small e-commerce platforms, DNSSEC provides added assurance that sensitive information is routed correctly and securely to its intended destination.

Education and awareness are also key to successful DNSSEC deployment in smaller environments. Many users are unfamiliar with DNSSEC and its role in securing DNS. Administrators should take the time to train staff and end-users on how DNSSEC protects them, what errors might appear if validation fails, and how to report issues. This helps create a security-conscious culture where users understand the importance of DNS integrity and the mechanisms in place to protect them.

Finally, small networks that deploy DNSSEC contribute to the broader security of the global internet. DNSSEC adoption has been steadily increasing, but there are still many zones and networks that operate without this critical protection. By signing their zones and validating incoming DNS queries, small networks strengthen the overall DNSSEC ecosystem, making it more difficult for attackers to exploit unsecured segments of the DNS.

Although small networks may face resource constraints and operational challenges, the tools and best practices available today make DNSSEC deployment increasingly accessible. By taking a measured approach—starting with enabling DNSSEC on externally hosted zones, deploying validating resolvers internally, and gradually building operational expertise—small organizations can enhance their resilience against a range of DNS-based threats and better safeguard their digital assets.

DNSSEC in Enterprise Environments

Implementing DNSSEC in enterprise environments introduces a new level of security to the organization's infrastructure, but it also comes with additional layers of complexity, scale, and operational responsibility. Enterprises typically operate large, distributed networks, host critical applications, and manage numerous domains and subdomains across multiple business units or regions. The DNS infrastructure in such settings often supports internal and external services, including web platforms, email systems, VPN access, cloud applications, and customer-facing services. Given the critical nature of these operations, enterprises are increasingly recognizing DNSSEC as a key component of their overall cybersecurity strategy, ensuring data authenticity and integrity across their DNS ecosystem.

The first consideration in deploying DNSSEC within an enterprise is the evaluation of the existing DNS infrastructure. Large organizations frequently manage hybrid environments consisting of in-house DNS servers, cloud-based DNS services, and third-party DNS hosting providers. Some enterprises run multiple authoritative DNS servers in different geographic locations to ensure high availability and low-latency responses for global users. The enterprise must decide whether to implement DNSSEC on-premises for internally hosted zones, rely on DNSSEC-enabled cloud services for external domains, or adopt a hybrid approach that leverages both.

Enterprises managing their own authoritative servers often use DNS software such as BIND, NSD, or Microsoft DNS Server, which all support DNSSEC capabilities. Deploying DNSSEC begins with the generation of cryptographic keys, typically both a Zone Signing Key (ZSK) and a Key Signing Key (KSK), for each zone under the enterprise's control. Each domain and subdomain that requires DNSSEC protection must be signed, and public keys must be published via DNSKEY records. The deployment of DNSSEC at this scale requires careful key management policies, including secure key storage, regular ZSK rollovers, and coordinated KSK rollovers to maintain the chain of trust between enterprise zones and their parent zones at the registry level.

Large enterprises often manage a portfolio of domains, sometimes numbering in the hundreds or thousands, including internal zones that are not publicly visible but are critical for internal communication, such as Active Directory zones. For internal DNSSEC implementations, enterprises typically configure private trust anchors for internal zones, as these may not be linked to the public DNS hierarchy. In contrast, for public-facing domains, DS records must be submitted to external registrars and parent zones to ensure proper integration into the public

DNSSEC trust chain. Managing DS records across multiple domains requires automation or well-documented procedures to reduce the risk of misconfigurations that could disrupt DNS resolution.

Beyond signing authoritative zones, enterprise DNSSEC deployments also require the deployment of DNSSEC-validating resolvers within the network. Large organizations often deploy multiple recursive resolvers across data centers, regional offices, and remote locations. These resolvers must be configured to validate DNSSEC signatures using the root trust anchor, which is typically embedded by default in modern resolver software. By ensuring that all outbound DNS queries from the enterprise network pass through validating resolvers, the organization protects users from forged DNS responses and external cache poisoning attempts.

One of the key operational challenges in enterprise DNSSEC deployments is ensuring that DNSSEC scales efficiently with the network. Signing large zones with thousands or millions of records generates a substantial number of RRSIG records, which increase the size of DNS responses. Enterprises must ensure that their network infrastructure—including firewalls, load balancers, intrusion detection systems, and any middleboxes—supports EDNS0 and accommodates DNS packets larger than 512 bytes. Misconfigured network appliances may drop or truncate large DNS responses, leading to resolution failures and degraded service availability. It is essential to conduct thorough testing and tune network configurations to allow seamless transport of DNSSEC-protected messages.

Enterprises must also address performance and redundancy considerations. Given that DNSSEC introduces additional computational overhead due to cryptographic operations such as signature generation and validation, organizations often deploy redundant DNS servers with load balancing to distribute the query load effectively. Implementing DNSSEC in globally distributed environments may also require signing zones in multiple regional data centers and synchronizing signed zone files across locations. Automation tools, such as OpenDNSSEC or vendor-specific DNSSEC management platforms, are crucial for handling repetitive tasks like key rollovers and zone resigning, reducing the risk of human error in complex environments.

DNSSEC in enterprise environments has a significant role in regulatory compliance and risk management strategies. Many industries, including finance, healthcare, and government sectors, are subject to regulations that emphasize the protection of DNS infrastructure as part of a broader cybersecurity framework. For example, regulatory bodies may require that DNS traffic is protected against known attacks, including DNS spoofing and redirection. By implementing DNSSEC, enterprises can demonstrate compliance with these requirements and provide evidence that measures are in place to protect DNS integrity.

Incident response and monitoring are also critical components of DNSSEC deployments at the enterprise level. Security teams must integrate DNSSEC validation logs and metrics into their security information and event management (SIEM) systems to detect anomalies, such as a sudden increase in bogus responses or validation failures. These alerts may indicate potential attacks, misconfigurations, or expired signatures within the DNSSEC infrastructure. Regular audits of key management practices, signature validity periods, and resolver configurations are necessary to ensure continuous DNSSEC effectiveness and to prevent downtime caused by expired keys or invalid signatures.

In addition to external-facing zones, enterprises often leverage DNSSEC internally to secure critical business services such as directory services, VPN access points, and cloud-based applications. As enterprises increasingly adopt hybrid cloud architectures, integrating DNSSEC with private cloud DNS environments becomes essential. Solutions like Amazon Route 53, Azure DNS, and Google Cloud DNS offer built-in DNSSEC capabilities that can be integrated with the organization's larger DNSSEC deployment strategy. Enterprises must establish standardized policies to ensure that DNSSEC is consistently deployed and maintained across both on-premises and cloud environments.

The benefits of DNSSEC in enterprise environments extend beyond securing DNS queries. By protecting against forged DNS data, enterprises can prevent phishing attacks, domain hijacking attempts, and service redirections aimed at exploiting users or stealing credentials. DNSSEC adds a layer of trust to online interactions, helping to protect employees, partners, and customers who rely on the organization's domains for communication and transactions.

Ultimately, the successful deployment of DNSSEC in enterprise environments depends on careful planning, automation, ongoing management, and collaboration between network teams, security teams, and domain administrators. While the scale and complexity of enterprise networks present challenges, the security benefits of DNSSEC and its ability to protect critical services and sensitive data make it a valuable investment in strengthening the organization's overall cybersecurity posture. As DNSSEC adoption continues to grow globally, enterprises that implement and maintain DNSSEC effectively will be better positioned to defend against increasingly sophisticated cyber threats targeting DNS infrastructure.

DNSSEC Deployment Best Practices

Deploying DNSSEC is a significant step toward securing the DNS infrastructure, but successful implementation requires careful planning, proper execution, and ongoing management. Organizations must follow a set of best practices to ensure that their DNSSEC deployment not only protects against common DNS threats but also operates smoothly without introducing avoidable risks or disruptions. A poorly implemented DNSSEC configuration can result in outages, broken trust chains, and a false sense of security. Best practices help maintain operational stability while maximizing the security benefits that DNSSEC offers.

The first best practice is to thoroughly assess the existing DNS environment before beginning the deployment. Administrators should identify all zones that the organization manages and classify them as either internal or external. Each zone must be reviewed to determine whether it will be signed, which key management policies will apply, and how DS records will be submitted to parent zones where necessary. During this assessment, administrators should also ensure that their DNS software, whether it is BIND, PowerDNS, NSD, Microsoft DNS Server, or a cloud-based DNS service, fully supports DNSSEC. Any legacy systems or network appliances that do not support DNSSEC-compliant responses should be upgraded or replaced to prevent compatibility issues.

Generating and managing cryptographic keys is one of the most critical components of DNSSEC deployment. It is considered best practice to separate the Key Signing Key (KSK) and Zone Signing Key (ZSK), where the KSK signs the DNSKEY record set, and the ZSK signs the remaining records in the zone. The KSK should be stored more securely and rotated less frequently, as it is the key linked to the parent zone via the DS record. The ZSK, which is used more regularly, should be rolled over at intervals that balance operational overhead with security needs. Automating key rollovers with tools such as OpenDNSSEC or BIND's inline signing feature helps reduce the chances of human error, which can result in outages caused by missing or outdated signatures.

Secure key storage is essential in DNSSEC deployments. Private keys, particularly KSKs, should be protected within Hardware Security Modules (HSMs) or secured servers with strict access controls. Restricting access to key material, limiting the number of administrators who can handle keys, and implementing key management policies aligned with security frameworks such as NIST recommendations are crucial steps to safeguarding DNSSEC's trust model. Additionally, key management processes should include regular audits to verify key integrity, proper storage practices, and compliance with the organization's broader security policies.

Another best practice is to implement comprehensive monitoring and alerting systems for the DNSSEC-enabled infrastructure. Signature expiration is a common cause of DNS resolution failures in signed zones. Administrators must monitor the validity periods of RRSIG records to ensure signatures are refreshed before expiration. Automated monitoring tools can detect if a signature is about to expire or has already expired, triggering alerts so that the issue can be corrected before it impacts availability. Similar monitoring should be in place for DS records, key rollovers, and unexpected validation failures, as these events may indicate operational errors or malicious activity targeting the DNSSEC deployment.

DNSSEC significantly increases the size of DNS responses due to the inclusion of RRSIG, DNSKEY, and DS records. Best practices recommend testing the network path to ensure that DNS packets larger than 512 bytes are transmitted successfully. This may require verifying that routers, firewalls, load balancers, and intrusion prevention systems support EDNS0 and are configured to handle larger UDP payloads or fallback to TCP when necessary. Failure to do so can result in fragmented or truncated DNS responses, leading to resolution failures for end users.

Another key practice is ensuring redundancy and resilience in the DNS infrastructure. DNSSEC imposes additional computational requirements on authoritative servers and resolvers due to signature generation and validation processes. Deploying multiple authoritative servers across geographically diverse locations, combined with load balancing and failover mechanisms, helps distribute the workload and enhances availability. Enterprises and service providers should also ensure that validating resolvers have redundant configurations and are placed strategically within the network to reduce latency and maintain high performance.

Documentation and change management are essential components of DNSSEC best practices. Every change related to DNSSEC, such as key rollovers, DS record submissions, and zone re-signing, should be meticulously documented and communicated to all relevant teams. Change control procedures should include pre-deployment testing, rollback plans, and clear timelines to coordinate activities such as KSK rollovers with parent zone operators. Organizations should also document their policies regarding key lengths, algorithm selection, rollover frequencies, and trust anchor configurations.

Choosing appropriate cryptographic algorithms is another critical best practice. While DNSSEC supports a variety of algorithms, administrators should select algorithms that balance security with performance. RSA with SHA-256 is still widely used, but elliptic curve algorithms such as ECDSA P-256 are increasingly recommended for their smaller key sizes and faster processing times. The choice of algorithm may depend on regulatory requirements, system capabilities, and industry standards. Administrators should also monitor algorithm deprecation notices from IANA and other authoritative bodies to ensure that their DNSSEC configurations remain compliant with evolving cryptographic guidelines.

Training and awareness play a vital role in DNSSEC success. Network administrators, security teams, and helpdesk staff must be familiar with DNSSEC operations, troubleshooting procedures, and the potential impacts of validation failures. Regular training sessions, combined with tabletop exercises simulating DNSSEC-related incidents, help prepare teams to respond effectively to both routine issues and security incidents. It is also beneficial to educate stakeholders and users about the value of DNSSEC, especially in organizations where DNS services are critical to business operations.

Finally, DNSSEC deployment should be incremental and carefully staged. Organizations should begin by deploying DNSSEC on non-critical zones or in test environments to familiarize teams with key management and signing operations. Once operational confidence is established, DNSSEC can be rolled out to high-value domains and critical infrastructure. During this phased approach, administrators should validate DNSSEC functionality using tools such as Verisign's DNSSEC debugger, DNSViz, and other DNSSEC validators to ensure that each stage of deployment is correctly implemented.

By adhering to these best practices, organizations can minimize risks, reduce the likelihood of service disruptions, and maximize the benefits of DNSSEC. A well-planned and maintained DNSSEC deployment strengthens DNS integrity, prevents common attacks, and supports broader cybersecurity efforts to protect users and systems from evolving threats in the modern digital landscape.

DNSSEC Key Management

DNSSEC key management is a crucial aspect of maintaining a secure and reliable DNSSEC deployment. At its core, key management involves the generation, storage, usage, rollover, and eventual retirement of cryptographic keys used to sign DNS records. Without proper key management, DNSSEC can become a source of operational risk rather than a security asset. The integrity of the entire DNSSEC validation chain depends on the secure handling of these keys, as any compromise, loss, or misconfiguration can disrupt DNS resolution and expose organizations to security vulnerabilities.

DNSSEC utilizes two distinct types of cryptographic keys: the Key Signing Key (KSK) and the Zone Signing Key (ZSK). The KSK has the specific role of signing the DNSKEY record set within a zone, effectively securing the public keys published for that zone. The ZSK, on the other hand, is used to sign all other resource record sets (RRsets) in the zone, such as A, AAAA, MX, and TXT records. This separation provides operational flexibility and enhances security by limiting the scope of each key's use. The KSK is often stored with higher levels of protection and is rolled over less frequently, while the ZSK is rotated more regularly due to its more frequent use in signing general zone data.

The first step in DNSSEC key management is the secure generation of keys. Administrators must ensure that both KSK and ZSK are generated using a strong, well-supported cryptographic algorithm such as RSA/SHA-256 or ECDSA P-256. Key lengths should meet current security recommendations, balancing performance with cryptographic strength. For example, RSA keys are often 2048 bits or longer, while ECDSA keys can achieve equivalent security with shorter key lengths, reducing DNS response sizes and improving efficiency.

Once generated, private keys must be stored securely to prevent unauthorized access. Best practices recommend storing private keys in a Hardware Security Module (HSM) or a secure, access-controlled server environment. Only authorized personnel should have access to the keys, and strict operational procedures should be enforced to prevent accidental exposure or misuse. Many organizations implement role-based access control (RBAC) to limit who can generate, use, and retire DNSSEC keys. Auditing mechanisms should also be in place to log key-related operations, including signing events and key rollovers.

DNSSEC key rollovers are a critical component of key management and must be performed regularly to maintain the security of the signed zone. The ZSK is typically rolled over more frequently than the KSK, with intervals determined by organizational policies and security requirements. A common ZSK rollover period might range from one to three months, depending on the sensitivity of the zone and regulatory considerations. The rollover process involves generating a new ZSK, re-signing the zone, and publishing both the old and new ZSKs in the DNSKEY RRset for a transitional period. This overlap allows resolvers with cached signatures generated by the old ZSK to continue validating responses until the old signatures expire and the new ZSK fully takes over.

The KSK rollover is a more complex process, as it affects the chain of trust with the parent zone. When a KSK is rolled over, a new DS record must be generated based on the new KSK and submitted to the parent zone registry. This submission links the child zone's new KSK to the parent zone's trust chain, ensuring that DNS resolvers can continue validating the zone's DNSKEY RRset. Due to the external dependency on the parent zone, KSK rollovers are typically performed less frequently, such as once every one or two years, unless there is a compelling reason to roll over the key earlier, such as key compromise or a change in security policy.

Automating key rollovers and resigning processes is highly recommended. Tools like OpenDNSSEC or BIND's built-in inline signing feature can handle ZSK rollovers automatically, generating new keys, re-signing the zone, and updating DNSKEY records without requiring manual intervention. Automation reduces the risk of human error, which can lead to outages if records are not properly signed or if keys are not correctly published. However, KSK rollovers often still require manual steps to update the DS record in the parent zone, making coordination with registrars or registry operators essential.

Key management also involves managing the validity periods of RRSIG records. Every signature created during the signing process has an inception and expiration time. Administrators must ensure that signatures are refreshed before they expire to prevent resolvers from rejecting responses due to outdated signatures. Automated monitoring systems should be used to track signature lifetimes and alert administrators well in advance of impending expiration dates.

In addition to operational tasks, key retirement is another important aspect of key management. Once a key, particularly a ZSK, is no longer in use and all signatures generated by it have expired, the key should be securely removed from the zone and the key storage system. For KSKs, once the rollover process has completed and the new DS record is published and propagated, the old KSK can also be safely retired. Retired keys must be securely deleted, ensuring that private key material is not left accessible within the organization's infrastructure.

DNSSEC key management is further complicated in environments with multiple zones or large-scale deployments. Enterprises managing hundreds of zones may choose to implement shared keys for related zones or configure individual keys for each zone, depending on their operational model and risk appetite. Regardless of the approach, key lifecycles must be synchronized and well-documented to prevent misconfigurations that could break DNSSEC validation.

Another emerging consideration in key management is the potential impact of quantum computing on current cryptographic algorithms. Although quantum-resistant algorithms are not yet standardized for DNSSEC, organizations with long-term planning horizons should stay informed about developments in post-quantum cryptography. Future-proofing key management processes will become increasingly relevant as industry standards evolve.

Lastly, organizations should integrate DNSSEC key management into their broader cybersecurity and disaster recovery plans. Keys should be backed up securely, and recovery procedures should be in place to restore DNSSEC functionality in the event of system failures, accidental deletions, or security breaches. By adopting comprehensive and secure key management practices, organizations ensure the long-term success and resilience of their DNSSEC deployments. The keys underpinning DNSSEC are the linchpin of trust in the DNS ecosystem, and their proper management is fundamental to preserving the integrity and reliability of DNS data across the internet.

Key Rollover Procedures

Key rollover is an essential procedure within DNSSEC operations, ensuring that cryptographic keys used to sign DNS records remain secure and up to date. In DNSSEC, two types of keys are routinely rolled over: the Zone Signing Key (ZSK) and the Key Signing Key (KSK). Each serves a distinct role in the DNSSEC framework, and both require careful handling during rollover events to avoid breaking the chain of trust. A well-executed key rollover preserves DNS resolution integrity and helps to mitigate the risk of key compromise or cryptographic weaknesses over time.

The Zone Signing Key is typically rolled over more frequently than the KSK due to its regular use in signing the majority of a zone's records. The general recommendation is to roll over the ZSK every few months, depending on the security policy and risk assessment of the organization. The ZSK is responsible for signing all non-DNSKEY resource record sets within a zone, including A, AAAA, MX, TXT, and CNAME records. Frequent use increases its exposure, making periodic rollover a best practice to minimize risk. The Key Signing Key, in contrast, signs only the DNSKEY record set, which contains both the KSK and ZSK public keys. Because the KSK is tied to the Delegation Signer (DS) record in the parent zone, its rollover is more complex and occurs less frequently, often once every year or two.

The ZSK rollover procedure typically begins with generating a new ZSK. This can be done manually using DNSSEC management tools or automatically if the DNS software supports inline signing or automated key management, such as with OpenDNSSEC or BIND. Once the new ZSK is generated, the next step is to introduce it into the DNSKEY record set for the zone, where it coexists with the current ZSK during a pre-publication phase. This overlap is crucial because DNS resolvers may have cached DNS data signed by the existing ZSK, and introducing the new ZSK alongside the old ensures that both signatures will validate until the old records expire.

After both ZSKs are present in the DNSKEY RRset, the zone administrator begins re-signing the zone's data with the new ZSK. During this phase, each resource record set is signed with the new key, generating new RRSIG records. Both the old and new signatures can coexist temporarily, or administrators may opt to remove the old signatures once the new ones are fully in place. This dual-signing period ensures that validators that still rely on the old ZSK for validation can continue to resolve DNS records without issue. Once sufficient time has passed, typically determined by the Time-To-Live (TTL) values and resolver cache durations, the old ZSK is safely removed from the DNSKEY RRset, leaving only the new ZSK active.

The KSK rollover procedure is more complex due to its relationship with the parent zone and the necessity to update the DS record. Similar to the ZSK rollover, the process begins by generating a new KSK, which is then introduced into the zone's DNSKEY record set alongside the old

KSK during the pre-publication phase. The old KSK still signs the DNSKEY RRset at this stage. The next step is to submit a new DS record, derived from the new KSK, to the parent zone's registry. This DS record must be accepted and published by the parent zone operator to update the trust chain.

Once the new DS record is live in the parent zone and fully propagated, the zone administrator can re-sign the DNSKEY RRset with the new KSK and begin the process of retiring the old KSK. The overlap period is critical here as well, since resolvers may still be relying on the old DS record during cache expiration. After a safe waiting period, the old KSK is removed from the DNSKEY RRset, and the DS record for the old key is removed from the parent zone.

Communication and coordination with the parent zone operator or domain registrar are essential during KSK rollovers to avoid introducing errors in the DS record update. If the DS record does not match the child zone's active KSK, the chain of trust will be broken, causing validation failures and DNS resolution outages for the affected domain. To minimize such risks, many organizations schedule KSK rollovers during maintenance windows and follow strict change control procedures, including pre-rollover testing in staging environments.

Automation can simplify key rollover processes, especially for ZSKs. Tools like OpenDNSSEC and some DNS software solutions can automate the generation of new keys, dual-publish the old and new keys, re-sign the zone, and eventually remove the old keys once the rollover is complete. Automating these steps reduces human error, ensures consistent policy enforcement, and facilitates compliance with key management best practices.

Another important consideration during key rollover is monitoring and validation. DNS administrators should continuously monitor their zones for validation status using tools such as DNSViz, Zonemaster, or Verisign's DNSSEC debugger. These tools can detect problems such as missing signatures, incorrect DS records, or misconfigured DNSKEY records. Alerts should also be configured within DNS management systems to notify teams of signature expiration dates, failed validations, or incomplete rollover steps.

It is also important to recognize that key rollover introduces an operational window where both old and new keys coexist. During this period, careful attention must be paid to resolver behaviors, TTL expiration times, and the propagation of updated DNSKEY and DS records. Administrators should allow ample time for caches to clear and for updated information to propagate throughout the DNS hierarchy before fully decommissioning old keys.

Lastly, documentation is a critical part of the rollover procedure. Every step, from key generation to DS submission and key removal, should be thoroughly documented. Documentation ensures that the process can be repeated consistently for future rollovers and that new personnel can follow established protocols. Organizations should also include key rollover procedures in their disaster recovery plans to ensure that key management tasks can proceed smoothly even during incidents or staffing changes.

When properly executed, key rollovers maintain the integrity of DNSSEC-signed zones and ensure uninterrupted service. By following structured rollover procedures and adhering to best practices, organizations can minimize risk, preserve the trust chain, and maintain the resilience of their DNSSEC deployments.

Automating DNSSEC

Automating DNSSEC is a critical strategy for organizations aiming to manage DNSSEC deployments efficiently, securely, and at scale. DNSSEC introduces additional layers of complexity to the traditional DNS workflow, requiring the generation, maintenance, and rollover of cryptographic keys, the consistent signing of DNS zones, and the correct distribution of Delegation Signer records to parent zones. Manually managing these tasks in a dynamic environment, particularly when dealing with multiple domains or frequently changing DNS records, introduces significant operational overhead and increases the likelihood of human error. Automation provides a solution by streamlining these processes and ensuring that DNSSEC operates smoothly and reliably.

One of the most common areas where automation plays a role is in key management, specifically the creation and rollover of Zone Signing Keys (ZSKs) and Key Signing Keys (KSKs). Automating key rollovers ensures that new cryptographic keys are generated on schedule and that zone records are re-signed automatically without the need for constant manual intervention. Automated systems handle key pre-publication, dual-signing during rollover periods, and safe retirement of old keys after a sufficient caching interval has passed. Tools such as OpenDNSSEC, Knot DNS, and BIND's inline signing feature are widely used to automate these processes, helping organizations maintain compliance with security policies and best practices for cryptographic hygiene.

Automated DNSSEC tools not only manage key lifecycles but also handle zone signing itself. DNSSEC requires every resource record set within a zone to be signed with a valid signature (RRSIG record) that must be refreshed periodically before expiration. Automating zone signing ensures that signatures are always current, preventing service interruptions due to expired signatures. Many modern DNS servers support automatic re-signing of zones based on configurable intervals or expiration thresholds. These tools also automatically insert and update DNSKEY and RRSIG records in the zone file, reducing the administrative burden on network teams.

For organizations managing multiple zones or frequently updated DNS records, automated DNSSEC signing is particularly valuable. Large enterprises and service providers may have dynamic zones that are updated in near real-time, such as for load balancers, content delivery networks, or cloud-based services. Manual re-signing in such environments would not be feasible. Automated DNSSEC solutions can detect changes to the zone file, sign the updated records immediately, and publish the zone without manual input. This enables administrators to maintain a secure DNS infrastructure even in fast-moving operational environments.

Automation also plays a crucial role in maintaining the chain of trust between zones and their parent domains. When rolling over a KSK, organizations must update the corresponding DS record in the parent zone to maintain the integrity of the DNSSEC trust chain. Some registrars and TLD operators offer APIs that allow automated DS record submission as part of a fully integrated DNSSEC management workflow. By combining DNSSEC automation tools with registrar APIs, organizations can ensure that KSK rollovers and DS record updates are executed in a coordinated, timely, and error-free manner.

Monitoring and alerting systems can also be integrated into the automated DNSSEC framework. Automation tools often provide hooks or logs that feed into Security Information and Event Management (SIEM) systems or custom dashboards. Administrators can set up alerts to notify them of failed signing attempts, upcoming signature expirations, unexpected key rollovers, or validation failures detected by external resolvers. This proactive monitoring ensures that DNSSEC-related issues are identified and addressed before they result in service disruptions.

Automating DNSSEC extends beyond the authoritative DNS infrastructure to recursive resolvers as well. Validating resolvers require a trusted root key or trust anchor to perform DNSSEC validation. Automated trust anchor management, as specified in RFC 5011, allows resolvers to update their trust anchors automatically when the root zone's KSK is rolled over. This eliminates the need for manual trust anchor updates and ensures that resolvers continue to validate DNSSEC responses without interruption, even when upstream trust anchors change.

Many DNSSEC automation solutions are compatible with broader DevOps and Infrastructure as Code (IaC) practices. For instance, DNSSEC key management and zone signing tasks can be integrated into configuration management tools like Ansible, Puppet, or Chef. This allows organizations to apply consistent DNSSEC configurations across multiple environments and automate deployment pipelines for DNS infrastructure. Automation ensures that DNSSEC policies are reproducible, consistent, and version-controlled, reducing configuration drift and simplifying disaster recovery efforts.

Security is a major consideration when automating DNSSEC. Automated systems must ensure that private keys are securely stored and accessed only by authorized processes. Hardware Security Modules (HSMs) or secure software-based key vaults are often integrated into the automation workflow to protect private keys during signing operations. These secure environments allow signing processes to occur within controlled and audited systems, maintaining the integrity and confidentiality of key material even in fully automated environments.

Another important factor in DNSSEC automation is scalability. As organizations grow or add new services and domains, automated DNSSEC workflows can scale to accommodate additional zones with minimal manual input. Automation platforms can be configured to detect new zones, generate appropriate cryptographic keys, sign the zones, and automatically submit DS records where applicable. This scalability is critical for service providers and enterprises that manage a large portfolio of domains, helping them to maintain DNSSEC adoption without overwhelming administrative resources.

Automation also reduces the potential for human error, which is a leading cause of DNSSEC-related outages. Common mistakes such as forgetting to re-sign zones, incorrectly configuring DNSKEY or DS records, or missing key rollover windows can lead to DNSSEC validation failures and service disruptions. Automation enforces operational discipline, ensuring that tasks occur consistently and according to policy, reducing the likelihood of outages due to misconfigurations or overlooked processes.

Automating DNSSEC allows organizations to focus on strategic objectives rather than the repetitive and technical tasks associated with cryptographic key management and zone signing. It enables faster rollouts of DNSSEC across multiple domains, improves incident response times, and enhances overall DNS security. Whether managing a single critical domain or hundreds of zones across a distributed network, automation provides the tools necessary to maintain a resilient, secure, and operationally efficient DNSSEC deployment. In an environment where DNS integrity is crucial to maintaining trust in online communications, automating DNSSEC has become a standard practice for organizations aiming to protect both internal and external DNS services at scale.

DNSSEC and IPv6

The adoption of IPv6 and the deployment of DNSSEC are two critical advancements that support the modern internet's scalability and security. While they are separate technologies serving different purposes, they are inherently complementary and together contribute to a more robust and secure internet infrastructure. IPv6 addresses the problem of IP address exhaustion by vastly expanding the number of available addresses, while DNSSEC focuses on securing the integrity and authenticity of DNS responses through cryptographic signatures. As the world transitions from IPv4 to IPv6, understanding how DNSSEC integrates with IPv6 environments is increasingly important for network administrators and organizations.

IPv6 expands the available address space from approximately four billion IPv4 addresses to an almost inexhaustible pool of 340 undecillion addresses. This massive increase supports the rapid growth of devices, services, and applications on the internet, enabling everything from large-scale cloud services to the Internet of Things. With this expansion comes a greater reliance on DNS to resolve human-readable domain names to IPv6 addresses, represented by AAAA records. Just as DNS is essential for resolving IPv4 addresses through A records, DNS is equally critical in IPv6 networks, where resolving AAAA records is a fundamental part of everyday network operations.

DNSSEC plays a vital role in protecting the resolution of both IPv4 and IPv6 addresses. Without DNSSEC, the DNS remains vulnerable to attacks such as cache poisoning, spoofing, and man-in-the-middle attacks, regardless of the IP version in use. Attackers could manipulate DNS responses to redirect traffic intended for legitimate IPv6 addresses to rogue destinations, placing users and systems at risk. By signing DNS responses with DNSSEC, organizations can guarantee that the AAAA records returned during resolution are authentic and have not been tampered with in transit. The cryptographic assurance provided by DNSSEC is equally critical when deploying IPv6 infrastructure, especially as the expanded address space introduces new operational and security challenges.

Deploying DNSSEC in an IPv6 environment follows the same principles as in an IPv4-only environment. The authoritative DNS server for a domain signs all its resource record sets, including AAAA records, using private keys. The corresponding digital signatures are included in RRSIG records, which are served alongside the AAAA records. When a resolver queries for an IPv6 address, it will receive the signed AAAA record and verify the RRSIG signature using the DNSKEY record retrieved from the same zone. The validation process follows the established DNSSEC chain of trust, starting from the root zone and moving downward through parent and child zones via DS and DNSKEY records.

One operational consideration in DNSSEC-enabled IPv6 environments is the management of the larger data payloads that both technologies introduce. IPv6 addresses are longer than their IPv4 counterparts, which increases the size of DNS responses containing AAAA records. DNSSEC further adds to this size by including RRSIG, DNSKEY, and potentially NSEC or NSEC3 records in DNS responses. The combined effect can lead to DNS message sizes that exceed the 512-byte limit imposed by traditional UDP-based DNS. To accommodate this, DNS software and network devices must fully support the Extension Mechanisms for DNS (EDNS0) to handle larger UDP packets or fallback to TCP when necessary. Organizations must ensure that their networks are properly configured to avoid packet truncation or dropped responses that can cause resolution failures.

IPv6's expanded address space also affects zone signing practices. With IPv4, administrators could feasibly control and monitor a relatively small range of IP addresses, but IPv6 subnets are much larger, and auto-configuration mechanisms such as SLAAC (Stateless Address Autoconfiguration) generate IPv6 addresses dynamically. As a result, DNSSEC's role in confirming the authenticity of AAAA records becomes even more valuable in IPv6 deployments. Without DNSSEC, attackers could exploit IPv6's vast address space to inject malicious records or leverage misconfigurations to compromise systems relying on IPv6 name resolution.

Another factor that strengthens the connection between DNSSEC and IPv6 is their alignment with modern security frameworks. Many government and industry cybersecurity policies now recommend or mandate the use of both IPv6 and DNSSEC. For example, several national governments require public-sector websites and services to be reachable over IPv6 and to implement DNSSEC to secure DNS operations. This combination is seen as a baseline for resilient, future-proof network design, supporting both address scalability and data authenticity in DNS.

While DNSSEC functions identically across IPv4 and IPv6 environments, organizations must also ensure that their recursive resolvers are configured to validate signatures for both A and AAAA records. Modern resolver software typically handles this automatically, but administrators should verify that DNSSEC validation is active and functioning correctly on all systems. Regular testing and monitoring using tools such as DNSViz or Verisign's DNSSEC debugger can help ensure that both IPv4 and IPv6 queries receive validated responses.

Enterprises that operate dual-stack networks, supporting both IPv4 and IPv6 simultaneously, face additional operational complexity. DNSSEC simplifies this challenge by providing a consistent security mechanism for DNS responses regardless of the IP protocol. Whether a resolver queries for an A record or a AAAA record, DNSSEC ensures that both responses are subject to the same cryptographic validation, reducing the risk of selective DNS attacks targeting one protocol over the other.

The transition to IPv6 also provides an opportunity for organizations to modernize their DNS operations and fully integrate DNSSEC into their infrastructure. As new IPv6 subnets and services are deployed, administrators can design DNS architectures that include DNSSEC from the outset, avoiding the need to retrofit security onto existing zones later. By building security into the DNS layer from the beginning of IPv6 adoption, organizations enhance their resilience to DNS threats and support secure communication across both internal and public networks.

DNSSEC and IPv6 also contribute to the trust model necessary for emerging technologies and services. For example, IoT deployments using IPv6 for device communication rely heavily on secure DNS to protect device-to-device and device-to-cloud interactions. In these scenarios, DNSSEC provides an additional safeguard against tampering and redirection attempts, ensuring that IoT endpoints communicate with legitimate services. Likewise, enterprises adopting IPv6 to support remote workforces, cloud services, or mobile applications will benefit from the integrity that DNSSEC brings to IPv6-enabled DNS queries.

The combination of DNSSEC and IPv6 is part of the broader evolution of the internet toward a more secure and scalable architecture. While each technology addresses a specific set of challenges—address exhaustion for IPv6 and data authenticity for DNSSEC—their integration is essential for building a trustworthy global network. Organizations that prioritize both technologies together position themselves to better defend against modern cyber threats while preparing for continued growth in internet-connected devices and services. By securing IPv6 address resolution with DNSSEC, network operators reinforce the reliability and integrity of communications in an increasingly complex and interconnected digital landscape.

DNSSEC and DANE (DNS-based Authentication of Named Entities)

DNSSEC, by itself, protects the integrity and authenticity of DNS data, ensuring that responses to DNS queries have not been tampered with and originate from the correct authoritative source. However, DNSSEC's functionality can be extended beyond traditional DNS validation to play a role in securing other protocols, including Transport Layer Security (TLS). This extension is realized through DANE, the DNS-based Authentication of Named Entities protocol. DANE leverages DNSSEC's cryptographic guarantees to allow domain owners to publish TLS certificate information directly in DNS. By doing so, DANE provides an additional layer of trust for TLS-enabled services such as HTTPS websites, email servers, and other applications relying on TLS or SSL for secure communications.

DANE was created to address several shortcomings of the current Public Key Infrastructure (PKI) system, which depends on a network of certificate authorities (CAs) to issue and validate digital certificates. While CAs have traditionally played a vital role in securing online services, their centralized nature has introduced systemic risks. History has shown that compromised or rogue certificate authorities can issue fraudulent certificates, enabling attackers to impersonate legitimate services. DANE reduces reliance on external CAs by empowering domain owners to assert which certificates or certificate fingerprints should be trusted for their services, using DNSSEC to secure and validate these assertions.

The cornerstone of DANE is the TLSA record, a new DNS resource record type introduced specifically for use with this protocol. The TLSA record binds a TLS certificate or public key to a domain name and port number combination, enabling clients to verify TLS connections using data obtained from DNS. Since the DNS data is protected by DNSSEC, clients can be assured that the TLSA record is authentic and has not been modified in transit. TLSA records specify the matching type, selector, and usage parameters that guide the client on how to interpret the record and what parts of the certificate chain to validate.

For example, an organization operating a secure website can publish TLSA records that specify the exact public key or certificate expected for the HTTPS service on port 443. When a user's browser or client queries the DNS for the domain, the resolver will retrieve the TLSA record alongside the A or AAAA records. The resolver will validate the TLSA record using DNSSEC's cryptographic chain of trust, ensuring that the information originates from the authoritative source. The client can then compare the TLS certificate presented by the server during the TLS handshake against the authenticated TLSA record data. If the information matches, the connection is trusted; if it does not, the client can reject the connection.

DANE's potential extends beyond websites to services like SMTP servers, which are notoriously vulnerable to man-in-the-middle attacks due to the lack of widespread TLS certificate validation between mail servers. With DANE, organizations can publish TLSA records for their mail servers, binding certificates directly to MX hostnames. This prevents attackers from successfully using fraudulent certificates to intercept or tamper with email delivery. By relying on DNSSEC-secured TLSA records, DANE strengthens email transport security and reduces the risk of email spoofing, phishing, and data interception.

Another significant advantage of DANE is its ability to work alongside or independently of traditional PKI. In scenarios where PKI is still required, DANE can be used to specify which certificate authority is allowed to issue certificates for a domain. Alternatively, DANE allows for PKI-independent usage, where the domain owner publishes self-signed certificates in DNS, enabling clients to validate connections without relying on third-party certificate authorities at all. This flexibility allows organizations to design security policies that align with their specific risk models and operational needs.

For DANE to be effective, DNSSEC validation must be enforced at the client side, and resolvers must support DNSSEC and TLSA queries. Modern DNS resolver software such as Unbound and BIND can perform DNSSEC validation and return validated TLSA records to clients. While adoption has been slower on the application layer, various email servers, browsers, and TLS libraries are beginning to integrate DANE support to enhance secure communications.

Operationally, deploying DANE starts with ensuring that DNSSEC is fully implemented on the domain. Without DNSSEC, TLSA records lack the cryptographic validation necessary to prevent tampering, rendering them insecure and ineffective. Once DNSSEC is operational, administrators can generate TLSA records based on the public key or certificate in use, following the guidelines provided in RFC 6698. These records are then published in DNS alongside other resource records and automatically secured by DNSSEC's zone-signing process.

The maintenance of TLSA records must be aligned with certificate lifecycle management. When a certificate is renewed, reissued, or replaced, the corresponding TLSA record must be updated to reflect the new information. Automated tools can streamline this process by generating new TLSA records whenever certificates are updated and ensuring that the signed DNS zone reflects the changes promptly. Neglecting to update TLSA records can result in failed validations, disrupting access to secured services.

DANE adoption is steadily growing, particularly in sectors where data confidentiality and integrity are paramount, such as financial services, government agencies, and healthcare providers. By leveraging DNSSEC to distribute certificate information, DANE enhances the trustworthiness of TLS communications and mitigates risks associated with compromised certificate authorities or misissued certificates. It is a step toward a more decentralized and resilient internet security model, aligning well with modern principles of zero trust and defense in depth.

Ultimately, DNSSEC and DANE form a powerful combination, extending DNSSEC's assurances of data authenticity to broader applications across the internet. As DNSSEC adoption expands, DANE stands to become a cornerstone in securing the TLS ecosystem, providing organizations and users with stronger guarantees of security and trust in an increasingly complex online environment.

DNSSEC and Email Security (DKIM, DMARC)

Email is one of the most widely used forms of communication on the internet, but it is also one of the most exploited vectors for cyberattacks, including phishing, spoofing, and spam campaigns. To combat these threats, the industry has developed multiple layers of email authentication protocols, notably DKIM (DomainKeys Identified Mail) and DMARC (Domain-based Message Authentication, Reporting, and Conformance). These mechanisms are designed to verify the legitimacy of emails by confirming that they originate from authorized servers and have not been tampered with during transit. However, while DKIM and DMARC greatly enhance email security, they both rely on the integrity of the DNS to function effectively. This is where DNSSEC becomes an indispensable partner in securing email infrastructure.

DKIM is a method for email senders to sign their outgoing messages using a private key. The corresponding public key is published in the DNS as a TXT record under a specific subdomain (typically selector._domainkey.example.com). When a receiving mail server gets an email, it retrieves the sender's DKIM public key from the DNS and uses it to validate the DKIM signature embedded in the message headers. If the signature matches, it proves that the email was indeed sent by the domain owner and has not been altered in transit. However, if an attacker can manipulate DNS responses by performing a man-in-the-middle attack or cache poisoning, they could provide a forged DKIM public key and trick the recipient's server into trusting a malicious message. This vulnerability highlights why DNSSEC is crucial to DKIM's reliability.

DNSSEC ensures that the DKIM public key retrieved from DNS is authentic by cryptographically signing the DNS response. When a resolver queries for the DKIM TXT record, the DNSSEC validation process confirms that the data originated from the authoritative DNS server and has not been modified. By securing the distribution of DKIM keys with DNSSEC, organizations prevent attackers from injecting fake keys or altering DKIM information, which could otherwise compromise the authenticity of legitimate email communications.

DMARC builds on top of DKIM and SPF (Sender Policy Framework) to provide a policy-based mechanism that domain owners can use to instruct receiving servers on how to handle messages that fail authentication checks. DMARC records are also published as TXT records in the DNS (under the _dmarc subdomain). These records specify whether to reject, quarantine, or accept messages that do not pass DKIM or SPF validation, along with reporting instructions for failed messages. Just like DKIM records, DMARC records are vulnerable to tampering if the DNS is not secured. Attackers could attempt to alter a domain's DMARC policy to prevent legitimate rejection of fraudulent emails, potentially allowing spoofed messages to bypass protections.

By signing DMARC records with DNSSEC, organizations can guarantee that the policies governing their domain's email authentication are protected from manipulation. This ensures that recipients always receive the correct instructions on how to handle unauthorized emails, further strengthening defenses against spoofing and phishing attacks. For high-profile domains, such as financial institutions, government agencies, and large enterprises, this protection is critical in safeguarding customers and partners from sophisticated email-based threats.

The synergy between DNSSEC, DKIM, and DMARC provides a multi-layered defense strategy. DNSSEC safeguards the integrity of the underlying DNS infrastructure, DKIM verifies that emails are sent by authorized servers and remain unaltered, and DMARC enforces domain-level policies that dictate how non-compliant messages should be treated. Together, they significantly reduce the success rate of email spoofing and phishing attacks, which continue to be the leading cause of data breaches and cybercrime globally.

Beyond securing DNS records, DNSSEC also indirectly supports other advanced email security frameworks. For example, DANE for SMTP (DANE-SMTP) allows mail servers to use DNSSEC-validated TLSA records to enforce mandatory encryption between mail transfer agents (MTAs). Without DNSSEC, attackers could downgrade SMTP sessions to plaintext, bypassing Transport Layer Security (TLS) protections and exposing emails to interception. DNSSEC strengthens DANE-SMTP by ensuring that the TLSA records used to secure SMTP communications are trustworthy and resistant to tampering.

Operationally, implementing DNSSEC in tandem with DKIM and DMARC involves ensuring that all zones publishing related TXT records are DNSSEC-signed and that the DNS infrastructure is capable of serving and validating DNSSEC responses. This requires authoritative DNS servers to be configured for DNSSEC signing and recursive resolvers to be set up for DNSSEC validation. Organizations should also automate the monitoring of DNSSEC signatures to prevent signature expiration, which could inadvertently break DKIM or DMARC validation.

It is important to recognize that while DNSSEC enhances the security of DKIM and DMARC, it does not replace them. Each mechanism addresses a different part of the email security puzzle. DNSSEC protects the transport and integrity of DNS records, DKIM authenticates the content and sender of individual messages, and DMARC defines domain-level policies for handling suspicious emails. When combined, they create a powerful framework that closes many of the gaps that cybercriminals exploit.

As phishing techniques evolve to become more sophisticated, organizations must adopt layered defenses that address multiple points of vulnerability. Cybercriminals often exploit weaknesses in DNS to subvert email authentication protocols or leverage unprotected domains to send convincing spoofed emails. Deploying DNSSEC in conjunction with DKIM and DMARC makes it far more difficult for attackers to manipulate DNS records or impersonate trusted domains.

The combined deployment of these technologies also has reputational benefits. Organizations that fully implement DNSSEC, DKIM, and DMARC demonstrate a proactive commitment to cybersecurity, fostering greater trust with customers, partners, and regulatory bodies. In sectors like banking, healthcare, and e-commerce, where sensitive data is exchanged via email, the implementation of such protections is often viewed as a security baseline rather than an optional enhancement.

To maximize the effectiveness of this integrated approach, organizations should also participate in industry-led initiatives that promote strong email security practices. Several global coalitions, such as the Global Cyber Alliance and M3AAWG, encourage best practices for implementing DNSSEC, DKIM, and DMARC, providing tools, templates, and training to support deployment and compliance.

Ultimately, DNSSEC serves as a foundational security layer that reinforces the reliability of DKIM and DMARC records, ensuring that email security policies cannot be undermined at the DNS level. Together, these technologies harden the email ecosystem against some of the most prevalent and damaging threats in today's digital landscape, protecting users, organizations, and critical infrastructure from the risks posed by email fraud and cybercrime.

DNSSEC and IoT Security

The rapid proliferation of Internet of Things (IoT) devices has introduced new challenges and risks to network security, especially as these devices increasingly depend on DNS to communicate with cloud services, APIs, and other endpoints. From industrial control systems and medical devices to smart home gadgets and autonomous vehicles, IoT systems rely heavily on DNS to resolve hostnames and access critical resources. However, the traditional DNS protocol, without additional security layers, is highly susceptible to attacks such as DNS spoofing, cache poisoning, and man-in-the-middle attacks. These vulnerabilities make IoT ecosystems prime targets for exploitation. Integrating DNSSEC into IoT environments strengthens the security posture of these systems by ensuring that DNS responses can be authenticated, reducing the likelihood of successful DNS-based attacks against IoT devices and services.

IoT devices typically operate in resource-constrained environments where processing power, memory, and bandwidth are limited. Despite these limitations, most IoT devices need to perform DNS lookups to interact with cloud services or other components within distributed architectures. These queries often resolve hostnames to IP addresses for firmware updates, telemetry uploads, or command and control communications. In the absence of DNSSEC, attackers could easily manipulate DNS responses, redirecting IoT devices to malicious servers controlled by adversaries. Such redirection can enable attackers to deliver rogue firmware updates, hijack device communications, or integrate compromised devices into botnets.

By incorporating DNSSEC into IoT infrastructure, organizations can significantly reduce the risk of these types of attacks. DNSSEC ensures that DNS responses received by IoT devices are signed and verifiable. When DNSSEC is properly implemented, any forged or altered DNS data is detected during the validation process, and the invalid data is rejected. This prevents IoT devices from connecting to unauthorized endpoints based on fraudulent DNS responses, enhancing the resilience of IoT ecosystems against common DNS-related threats.

One of the primary advantages of DNSSEC in IoT deployments is its ability to provide a scalable and decentralized method of trust. Instead of relying solely on private certificate infrastructures or hardcoded trust relationships, IoT devices can leverage DNSSEC-validated DNS queries to authenticate server endpoints dynamically. This is especially valuable in large-scale IoT deployments involving thousands or millions of devices operating across diverse networks, where centralized trust models may not scale efficiently.

However, DNSSEC's benefits to IoT security also come with implementation challenges. Many IoT devices are designed with minimal processing capabilities, making it difficult for them to handle the additional computational overhead associated with DNSSEC validation. Performing signature verification on DNSSEC-signed responses requires cryptographic operations that may strain the limited resources of these devices. To address this challenge, a common approach is to delegate DNSSEC validation to upstream recursive resolvers that are DNSSEC-aware. These validating resolvers perform the cryptographic checks on behalf of the IoT devices and only forward validated DNS responses downstream. By offloading validation duties to trusted resolvers, organizations can secure IoT communications without burdening the devices themselves.

Another critical consideration is the secure bootstrapping of IoT devices. When a device is first deployed, it must securely establish connections to initial services such as provisioning servers, cloud platforms, or firmware repositories. DNSSEC can play a vital role in this process by ensuring that DNS lookups performed during device initialization are resistant to tampering. For instance, if an IoT device uses DNS to locate its cloud management endpoint, DNSSEC validation helps guarantee that the address retrieved is correct and has not been substituted by an attacker attempting to hijack the onboarding process.

Additionally, DNSSEC complements other IoT security mechanisms such as Mutual TLS (mTLS), hardware-based trust anchors, and signed firmware updates. While DNSSEC alone does not provide end-to-end encryption or device authentication, it acts as a crucial first line of defense against DNS-level attacks that could undermine these other security controls. By preventing attackers from intercepting or redirecting traffic at the DNS layer, DNSSEC ensures that IoT devices are reaching the correct, authorized endpoints before initiating secure sessions or downloading software updates.

As the number of connected IoT devices grows, many industries are adopting best practices and regulatory frameworks that include DNS security requirements. Sectors such as critical infrastructure, healthcare, automotive, and manufacturing increasingly mandate stronger DNS protections to safeguard IoT systems from disruption or compromise. DNSSEC is often recommended or required as part of these guidelines, reinforcing its role in the modern security landscape.

Furthermore, the use of DNSSEC in IoT networks can help organizations defend against supply chain attacks. Many IoT devices rely on third-party services for software updates, telemetry collection, and command issuance. By validating DNS responses using DNSSEC, organizations can reduce the risk of devices interacting with counterfeit servers introduced by attackers targeting these supply chains. This is particularly relevant in environments where IoT devices autonomously fetch updates or instructions without human oversight.

Operationally, deploying DNSSEC in IoT environments involves configuring both authoritative DNS servers and validating recursive resolvers. For IoT manufacturers and service providers, this means ensuring that all relevant zones hosting DNS records for device services are DNSSEC-signed. For organizations managing IoT fleets, it involves using or deploying resolvers capable of performing DNSSEC validation and monitoring for validation failures that could signal potential security issues or misconfigurations.

In hybrid environments where IoT devices communicate over both IPv4 and IPv6 networks, DNSSEC provides consistent protection regardless of the IP protocol in use. Whether IoT devices resolve A records for IPv4 or AAAA records for IPv6, DNSSEC ensures that the integrity of the DNS data is maintained, blocking unauthorized changes to address mappings that could facilitate attacks.

DNSSEC also offers future-proofing benefits as IoT ecosystems continue to evolve. As more advanced threats emerge, targeting everything from smart cities to industrial automation systems, organizations will need to layer multiple security mechanisms to protect critical IoT infrastructures. DNSSEC will remain a fundamental component of this multi-layered approach, helping to secure DNS communications, a vital and often-overlooked aspect of IoT operations.

Ultimately, DNSSEC's ability to authenticate DNS responses helps mitigate a wide range of attack vectors that threaten IoT deployments. By integrating DNSSEC into the security architecture of IoT systems, organizations can better defend against DNS-based attacks that could otherwise compromise device integrity, disrupt services, or expose sensitive data. In an increasingly connected world, where IoT devices play key roles in daily operations and critical infrastructure, strengthening DNS security through DNSSEC is a proactive and necessary measure to protect the future of IoT.

DNSSEC in Cloud Environments

As organizations increasingly migrate their infrastructure and services to the cloud, securing DNS operations in these environments has become a critical component of an effective cybersecurity strategy. Cloud platforms host a wide array of services, from web applications and APIs to virtual networks and hybrid workloads, all of which depend on DNS for reliable name resolution. The transition to cloud environments does not eliminate the vulnerabilities inherent in traditional DNS; in fact, it often introduces new challenges. DNSSEC, when integrated into cloud-based DNS services, provides essential protection by ensuring the authenticity and integrity of DNS data, preventing attackers from intercepting or tampering with DNS queries and responses.

Cloud service providers (CSPs) such as Amazon Web Services (AWS), Microsoft Azure, and Google Cloud Platform (GCP) have all incorporated DNSSEC into their managed DNS offerings. These platforms provide users with authoritative DNS services where zones can be hosted and configured directly within the cloud infrastructure. Organizations can create, manage, and scale their DNS zones alongside other cloud-native resources, simplifying the overall network management process. However, unless DNSSEC is enabled and configured correctly, cloud-hosted DNS zones remain vulnerable to traditional DNS attacks like cache poisoning and spoofing.

One of the advantages of implementing DNSSEC in cloud environments is the relative ease of deployment compared to on-premises setups. Major cloud providers have streamlined the process by offering automation and integration with other platform services. For example, AWS Route 53 allows customers to enable DNSSEC signing on public hosted zones through a few clicks in the management console. The cloud provider automatically handles key generation, signing of DNS records, and regular key rollover processes. Similarly, GCP Cloud DNS and Azure DNS provide options for enabling DNSSEC for hosted zones and assist with key management to reduce operational overhead for customers.

Despite these built-in features, organizations must still coordinate the publishing of Delegation Signer (DS) records with the parent domain registries. This is a critical step, as it establishes the chain of trust necessary for DNSSEC validation to work. Some cloud platforms integrate directly with domain registrars, allowing DS records to be submitted automatically. Others require administrators to export DS record data and manually configure it with their registrar. Failing to complete this step leaves the DNSSEC deployment incomplete, limiting its effectiveness.

A common characteristic of cloud environments is the dynamic nature of the infrastructure. Resources such as virtual machines, load balancers, containers, and services are frequently created, destroyed, or reconfigured to adapt to changing workloads. This dynamism demands a DNSSEC implementation that can accommodate frequent changes to DNS records. Automated DNSSEC signing, which cloud DNS services typically offer, plays a crucial role in ensuring that each DNS change is promptly and properly signed with valid cryptographic signatures. Without this automation, managing RRSIG record updates and key rotations in fast-changing cloud environments would be unmanageable.

DNSSEC in cloud environments is also vital for multi-cloud and hybrid-cloud architectures. Many organizations adopt a multi-cloud strategy to avoid vendor lock-in or to optimize services across different CSPs. In such scenarios, DNS records may be distributed across multiple cloud providers' DNS services or integrated with on-premises DNS infrastructure. DNSSEC provides a consistent security layer that applies to all these environments, ensuring that DNS responses are verifiable and trusted regardless of where the authoritative DNS zone resides.

Another key advantage of using DNSSEC in cloud environments is that it can be integrated with cloud-native security services to enhance incident detection and response. For instance, CSPs often offer monitoring tools, logging services, and security event management platforms. When DNSSEC is deployed, logs related to DNSSEC validation failures or anomalies in DNS traffic can be fed into security information and event management (SIEM) systems for real-time analysis. Alerts generated from these systems help security teams detect potential attacks, such as attempts to inject forged DNS responses or manipulate DNS records at the DNS infrastructure level.

The scalability and resilience provided by cloud-native DNSSEC solutions are particularly attractive to enterprises operating global services. By leveraging the distributed infrastructure of CSPs, organizations benefit from geographically redundant DNS servers with automated failover and load balancing capabilities. Combined with DNSSEC signing, this setup ensures that DNS queries are both secure and highly available, reducing latency for users worldwide while maintaining the integrity of DNS data.

However, organizations must also be mindful of certain operational challenges. While cloud providers handle much of the backend complexity, customers still bear responsibility for managing DNSSEC policies, including deciding when to initiate key rollovers for zones and ensuring that downstream systems, such as recursive resolvers, support DNSSEC validation. Additionally, organizations must validate that their applications and services are compatible with the increased DNS response sizes that result from DNSSEC signatures and key material. DNS queries from cloud environments must pass through virtual firewalls, network security groups, and other infrastructure components that may impose size limits on DNS packets. Ensuring that EDNS0 is supported across all components is necessary to prevent resolution failures due to packet truncation.

DNSSEC also enhances the security of API-driven cloud applications. Many cloud-based services rely on DNS to resolve service endpoints, both internally between microservices and externally for public APIs. By securing the DNS layer, DNSSEC helps prevent service disruptions caused by DNS tampering, such as directing API calls to malicious endpoints. This is particularly relevant in DevOps and CI/CD pipelines where automated tools and services depend on secure DNS resolution to interact with cloud-native resources.

Additionally, DNSSEC in cloud environments supports compliance efforts. Various regulatory frameworks, including GDPR, HIPAA, and ISO/IEC 27001, emphasize the need to protect data in transit and ensure system integrity. By deploying DNSSEC alongside other security controls in the cloud, organizations can demonstrate that they are taking proactive steps to secure the DNS infrastructure, helping meet regulatory and audit requirements.

As cloud-native environments continue to evolve, so too will the need for strong, integrated DNS security measures. The combination of DNSSEC with other cloud-native security technologies, such as DNS-based firewalls, web application firewalls (WAFs), and identity and access management (IAM) systems, creates a comprehensive security ecosystem that protects cloud-based applications and services against a wide array of threats. DNSSEC plays a foundational role in this ecosystem by safeguarding the DNS layer, which is central to the operation of virtually all internet-facing and internal cloud services.

Ultimately, DNSSEC in cloud environments provides organizations with a scalable, automated, and effective way to protect DNS infrastructure from tampering, reduce the risk of cyberattacks, and ensure the authenticity of DNS responses in dynamic, fast-paced cloud ecosystems. By taking full advantage of the DNSSEC capabilities offered by cloud providers, organizations strengthen the security of their cloud operations and contribute to the broader security of the internet as a whole.

DNSSEC for Critical Infrastructure

Critical infrastructure encompasses systems and assets essential for the functioning of a society and economy, including sectors such as energy, water, telecommunications, transportation, healthcare, and financial services. These industries rely heavily on secure and reliable communications networks to ensure their continuous operation and to safeguard public safety and national security. The Domain Name

System is a vital component of this communications backbone, providing the mechanism by which essential services locate and interact with one another. As such, the security of DNS within critical infrastructure environments is paramount. DNSSEC plays a fundamental role in fortifying this layer by protecting DNS queries and responses from manipulation, thereby ensuring the integrity and trustworthiness of communications.

In critical infrastructure, the consequences of DNS attacks can be catastrophic. A successful DNS spoofing or cache poisoning attack could redirect traffic from legitimate servers to malicious actors, disrupt operational technologies, cause downtime for essential public services, or serve as a launching point for further intrusions into sensitive systems. For example, if a DNS resolver serving a power grid operator were compromised, attackers could reroute monitoring systems, interfere with SCADA networks, or deny access to essential command-and-control systems. In sectors where system availability and data integrity are non-negotiable, securing DNS with DNSSEC becomes an operational necessity.

DNSSEC safeguards DNS operations by cryptographically signing DNS records, enabling resolvers to validate that the information they receive originates from an authoritative source and has not been altered in transit. In critical infrastructure, this functionality ensures that vital systems only receive authentic DNS data when resolving IP addresses for control systems, data centers, cloud services, or external partners. By rejecting forged or modified DNS responses, DNSSEC significantly reduces the risk of attackers exploiting the DNS layer to disrupt or compromise critical assets.

Implementing DNSSEC across critical infrastructure environments begins with securing the authoritative DNS zones that serve critical domains. Whether these zones resolve names for an emergency response system, a transportation control network, or financial clearinghouse systems, the integrity of their DNS data must be preserved. Administrators must ensure that these zones are properly signed using robust cryptographic algorithms, and that the corresponding DS records are submitted to the parent zones to maintain the chain of trust. For infrastructure operators, this means coordinating closely with registrars, parent domain owners, and regulatory bodies to ensure the entire DNSSEC deployment is aligned with broader industry security mandates.

Critical infrastructure sectors often operate hybrid environments where public DNS services coexist with private or internal DNS zones supporting isolated networks. DNSSEC's flexibility allows it to be deployed both externally for public-facing services and internally within segmented operational networks. For example, in an industrial environment, internal DNS zones used by ICS (Industrial Control Systems) or OT (Operational Technology) networks can be signed with DNSSEC, adding an additional layer of defense against insider threats or supply chain attacks that might target internal name resolution.

In regulated sectors such as energy or finance, the deployment of DNSSEC aligns with legal and compliance requirements aimed at ensuring national security and the resilience of essential services. Governments and regulatory agencies around the world increasingly advocate for or mandate DNSSEC implementation within critical infrastructure sectors. National cybersecurity frameworks and guidelines, including those from organizations like NIST, the European Union Agency for Cybersecurity (ENISA), and the International Telecommunication Union (ITU), highlight DNSSEC as a recommended or required control. Compliance with these guidelines helps organizations demonstrate due diligence and strengthen their cybersecurity posture.

DNSSEC also enhances the security of critical infrastructure supply chains. Many essential services rely on a complex web of third-party vendors, service providers, and partners who deliver hardware, software, or operational support. Ensuring that all external DNS queries, such as those involved in software updates, partner integrations, or external data exchanges, are validated with DNSSEC reduces the risk of supply chain attacks that manipulate DNS records to divert traffic to malicious endpoints.

Operationalizing DNSSEC in critical infrastructure requires a focus on automation and monitoring to reduce the risks associated with human error and resource constraints. Automated key management and zone signing solutions help ensure that cryptographic keys are rotated on schedule and that zone data is signed correctly without manual intervention. These systems reduce administrative overhead while minimizing the risk of expired signatures or incomplete rollovers that could disrupt operations.

Monitoring and alerting systems should be tightly integrated with DNSSEC deployments. Validation failures, anomalies in DNS traffic patterns, or sudden increases in bogus responses could indicate ongoing attacks or misconfigurations. Security operations centers (SOCs) managing critical infrastructure should incorporate DNSSEC validation logs into their SIEM platforms and incident response workflows to detect and respond to DNS-related threats in real-time.

Another essential component of DNSSEC deployments in critical infrastructure is resilience planning. Operators must design DNS architectures with redundancy, geographic distribution, and failover mechanisms to withstand both technical failures and deliberate attacks. Combining DNSSEC with anycast routing and globally distributed authoritative servers helps ensure that DNS queries are not only secure but also highly available under adverse conditions, such as DDoS attacks targeting DNS infrastructure.

While DNSSEC provides robust protection at the DNS layer, it should be part of a larger defense-in-depth strategy. In critical infrastructure environments, DNSSEC complements other controls such as network segmentation, zero trust architectures, endpoint protection, and strict access controls. DNSSEC ensures that the foundational trust in DNS resolution is preserved, enabling other security mechanisms to operate on the basis of reliable domain name resolution.

Organizations responsible for critical infrastructure should also prioritize stakeholder engagement and security awareness initiatives. System administrators, network engineers, and management teams must understand the importance of DNSSEC and its role in protecting essential services. Comprehensive documentation, training programs, and tabletop exercises simulating DNS-related incidents help ensure that staff can effectively manage DNSSEC deployments and respond to issues when they arise.

DNSSEC plays a pivotal role in safeguarding the networks and services that underpin modern society. By ensuring the authenticity and integrity of DNS data within critical infrastructure environments, DNSSEC protects against a wide range of cyber threats that could otherwise undermine essential public and private sector functions. In doing so, it strengthens national resilience, preserves public trust, and reinforces the stability of the global economy and the services people rely on every day.

DNSSEC Compliance and Policy Considerations

DNSSEC compliance and policy considerations have become increasingly relevant as organizations, governments, and industries seek to strengthen their cybersecurity postures and protect digital infrastructure against growing threats. While DNSSEC serves as a technical solution to secure DNS data through cryptographic signatures, its deployment and management must also align with regulatory frameworks, industry standards, and internal governance policies to ensure a comprehensive approach to DNS security.

One of the driving forces behind DNSSEC compliance is the recognition that DNS vulnerabilities pose significant risks to the confidentiality, integrity, and availability of critical services. Regulatory bodies and international organizations have incorporated DNSSEC into security standards, urging or mandating organizations to adopt it as part of a layered defense strategy. For example, the United States National Institute of Standards and Technology (NIST) recommends DNSSEC implementation in its cybersecurity frameworks, including SP 800-81, which provides technical guidance on securing DNS infrastructure. Similarly, the European Union Agency for Cybersecurity (ENISA) highlights DNSSEC in its recommendations for securing DNS services and mitigating threats such as cache poisoning and DNS spoofing.

From a policy perspective, DNSSEC deployment requires organizations to define clear roles, responsibilities, and operational procedures. A DNSSEC policy must specify how cryptographic keys are generated, stored, and rotated, as well as how DNS zones are signed and monitored. Policies should establish requirements for the separation of duties, ensuring that no single individual or team has unilateral control over critical DNSSEC key material. This principle of least privilege reduces the risk of insider threats and human error.

Compliance also demands that organizations integrate DNSSEC management into their broader risk management and security governance frameworks. This includes conducting regular audits to ensure that DNSSEC configurations are properly maintained, that cryptographic algorithms and key lengths adhere to current security recommendations, and that DS records are consistently published in parent zones. Organizations must also assess the potential impact of DNSSEC on system availability and performance, balancing security with operational requirements.

A common compliance challenge involves managing DNSSEC across multiple domains and registrars, particularly for organizations with large portfolios of domains or international operations. Policies must account for variations in registrar capabilities and regulatory requirements across jurisdictions. Some registrars offer automated DS record submissions and key rollover support, while others require manual processes that may introduce delays or inconsistencies. A strong DNSSEC policy must include standardized procedures for coordinating with registrars, ensuring that all domains under an organization's control are fully integrated into the DNSSEC trust chain.

The regulatory landscape surrounding DNSSEC is also evolving. In sectors such as finance, energy, healthcare, and government, regulatory bodies increasingly require organizations to implement DNSSEC to meet sector-specific security standards. For example, in the financial industry, DNSSEC is often cited as part of cybersecurity requirements aimed at protecting critical financial systems and customer data from DNS-related threats. In the healthcare sector, where patient privacy and data security are paramount, securing DNS with DNSSEC helps organizations comply with regulations such as HIPAA, which emphasize the need to safeguard electronic communications.

DNSSEC policy considerations extend to business continuity and disaster recovery planning. Organizations must define how DNSSEC keys and signing operations will be restored in the event of a system failure, cyberattack, or natural disaster. Backup and recovery processes should include the secure storage of cryptographic key material in geographically diverse and access-controlled environments. Additionally, incident response plans should address how to handle DNSSEC-related incidents, such as key compromises, validation failures, or DS record mismatches, to minimize operational disruptions and preserve the integrity of DNS services.

Another important consideration is the selection of cryptographic algorithms and key sizes. Compliance with best practices, such as those recommended by the Internet Assigned Numbers Authority (IANA) and NIST, dictates that organizations periodically review and update their cryptographic parameters to address advances in computing power and cryptanalysis. For example, while RSA with SHA-256 remains widely used, elliptic curve algorithms such as ECDSA P-256 are increasingly favored for their efficiency and shorter key lengths. A robust DNSSEC policy should document the organization's approved algorithms and procedures for algorithm migration when necessary.

DNSSEC compliance also intersects with privacy considerations, particularly in light of data protection regulations such as the General Data Protection Regulation (GDPR) in the European Union. While DNSSEC itself does not encrypt DNS queries or responses, it can help prevent attackers from injecting unauthorized content into DNS traffic, which could be used to harvest personal information or manipulate user behavior. Organizations must ensure that DNSSEC deployment does not inadvertently expose sensitive information through poorly configured DNS records or public key material. Policies should mandate regular reviews of DNS zone content to minimize the risk of unintentional data exposure.

Training and awareness are essential components of DNSSEC compliance. All personnel involved in DNS management, network security, and incident response should be trained on DNSSEC principles, deployment practices, and troubleshooting techniques. Compliance policies should include mandatory training programs, supplemented by ongoing education to keep teams informed of evolving DNSSEC standards and threat landscapes. Establishing a culture of security awareness helps ensure that DNSSEC operations are carried out diligently and in accordance with organizational policies.

Reporting and documentation are additional requirements in regulated environments. Organizations must maintain comprehensive records of DNSSEC-related activities, including key generation events, zone signing operations, DS record submissions, and validation logs. This documentation serves as evidence of compliance during regulatory audits and can aid in forensic investigations following security incidents. Policies should specify retention periods for DNSSEC-related records and ensure that documentation is securely stored and accessible to authorized personnel.

Global DNSSEC adoption rates, while steadily increasing, remain inconsistent across regions and industries. As part of compliance initiatives, organizations may also participate in industry collaborations, information sharing groups, and national or international cybersecurity initiatives that promote DNSSEC deployment. By aligning internal DNSSEC policies with broader industry efforts, organizations contribute to strengthening the global DNS ecosystem and enhancing collective resilience against DNS threats.

Ultimately, DNSSEC compliance and policy considerations must balance the need for security, operational efficiency, and regulatory adherence. DNSSEC is not simply a technical control but a strategic component of an organization's cybersecurity framework. It requires a holistic approach that integrates technical implementation with sound governance, risk management, and compliance practices. As cyber threats targeting the DNS layer continue to evolve, organizations that adopt comprehensive DNSSEC policies will be better positioned to protect their infrastructure, meet regulatory requirements, and preserve the trust and confidence of their stakeholders.

Common DNSSEC Implementation Pitfalls

Despite its critical role in securing DNS infrastructure, DNSSEC implementation is often fraught with challenges and pitfalls that can lead to service disruptions, broken validation chains, or incomplete protection. Many organizations, while aware of DNSSEC's security benefits, underestimate the operational complexities involved or overlook key steps in the deployment and maintenance process. These common pitfalls not only jeopardize the effectiveness of DNSSEC but may also inadvertently introduce risks that the organization intended to mitigate.

One of the most frequent mistakes is failing to complete the chain of trust by omitting the Delegation Signer (DS) record in the parent zone. When an organization signs its DNS zone with DNSSEC, the public keys are published as DNSKEY records within the zone. However, unless the corresponding DS record is properly submitted and published in the parent zone, validating resolvers will be unable to establish trust from the root zone down to the signed domain. This incomplete deployment leaves the DNSSEC-protected zone unverifiable by external resolvers, rendering the entire effort ineffective. Administrators may sign their zones correctly but then forget to coordinate with their domain registrar to update or maintain the DS record, breaking the validation chain.

Improper key management is another common pitfall. Organizations often neglect to plan for regular key rollovers, leaving cryptographic keys active for extended periods. This increases the risk that a private key could be compromised or that the algorithm in use becomes outdated or weakened. Conversely, poorly executed key rollovers can also lead to validation failures. For instance, removing an old Key Signing Key (KSK) or Zone Signing Key (ZSK) from the DNSKEY record set before all resolver caches have expired the old RRSIG records can result in clients failing to validate DNS responses. Organizations must follow best practices, including pre-publishing new keys, maintaining overlap periods, and monitoring resolver behavior before retiring old keys.

Another frequent issue is signature expiration. DNSSEC relies on digital signatures (RRSIG records) that have defined validity periods. If an administrator fails to monitor and refresh these signatures before they expire, resolvers will treat responses as invalid, leading to DNS resolution failures and potential service outages. This is particularly problematic for dynamic or frequently updated zones, where record changes trigger re-signing events. Many administrators rely on manual processes to manage signatures, increasing the likelihood of missing re-signing deadlines. Automated signing tools and key management platforms are available but are not always implemented, leaving organizations vulnerable to avoidable outages.

Misconfigured or inconsistent DNSSEC settings across different zones or environments also pose significant risks. For example, organizations with multiple domains or subdomains might sign some zones with DNSSEC while leaving others unsigned, creating gaps in protection. Inconsistent policies may result in parent zones that sign DS records for only certain child zones, fragmenting the chain of trust. Similarly, enterprises operating in hybrid environments, where some zones are hosted internally and others are delegated to cloud-based DNS services, may fail to apply uniform DNSSEC policies, leading to disparities in how DNS traffic is secured.

Another operational pitfall relates to inadequate monitoring and alerting. DNSSEC introduces new failure modes, such as cryptographic validation errors, DNSKEY and DS record mismatches, or NSEC/NSEC3-related issues in negative responses. Without comprehensive monitoring of DNSSEC validation results, administrators may be unaware of failures occurring at recursive resolvers. A lack of visibility into validation logs means that service disruptions might persist unnoticed until end-users report issues. Proactive monitoring using tools such as DNSViz, Zonemaster, and SIEM integrations is crucial for detecting and resolving DNSSEC-related problems in real-time.

The performance impact of DNSSEC is often overlooked as well. Signing zones increases DNS response sizes due to the additional DNSSEC records such as RRSIG, DNSKEY, and NSEC/NSEC3. If network devices, firewalls, or middleboxes along the DNS query path are not configured to support EDNS0 or to handle larger UDP packets, legitimate DNS responses may be truncated, resulting in failed queries or fallback to TCP, which can affect latency and user experience. Organizations frequently deploy DNSSEC without validating that their network infrastructure can accommodate these larger packet sizes, leading to resolution problems post-implementation.

DNSSEC misconfiguration can also lead to operational inefficiencies or vulnerabilities through poor algorithm selection. While older algorithms such as RSA/SHA-1 were widely used in earlier DNSSEC deployments, they are no longer recommended due to advances in cryptanalysis and growing computational inefficiencies. Some organizations continue to use outdated algorithms due to legacy systems or lack of awareness, putting the integrity of their DNSSEC deployment at risk. Modern best practices recommend using algorithms like RSA/SHA-256 or ECDSA P-256, which provide better security and smaller signature sizes.

Another pitfall lies in neglecting internal DNS zones. Many organizations focus exclusively on signing public-facing zones while leaving internal DNS zones, such as those used for Active Directory or operational technology networks, unsigned. This oversight ignores insider threats or lateral movement attacks, where adversaries operating within the internal network could manipulate DNS records to intercept traffic or target vulnerable systems. By signing internal zones with DNSSEC and configuring validating resolvers internally, organizations can extend protection to the entire DNS footprint.

Finally, a lack of training and organizational awareness is a persistent challenge. DNSSEC requires specialized knowledge to deploy and manage effectively, including understanding cryptographic principles, DNS resolver behavior, and trust chain mechanics. In many cases, DNS administrators or IT teams implement DNSSEC without fully understanding the nuances of key rollover procedures, validation workflows, or troubleshooting techniques. Without ongoing training and a culture of security awareness, DNSSEC configurations may be left in an insecure or suboptimal state.

To avoid these pitfalls, organizations should take a holistic approach to DNSSEC deployment, integrating it into their broader cybersecurity and governance frameworks. This includes establishing clear DNSSEC management policies, automating routine processes, ensuring consistent configurations across all DNS zones, and maintaining operational visibility into DNSSEC performance and validation health. By proactively addressing common implementation challenges, organizations can fully realize the benefits of DNSSEC, securing the DNS layer against an ever-evolving landscape of cyber threats.

Troubleshooting DNSSEC Issues

Troubleshooting DNSSEC issues requires a methodical approach due to the multiple layers of cryptographic operations, key management procedures, and resolver interactions involved in the DNSSEC validation process. While DNSSEC is designed to enhance security by protecting DNS data against tampering and forgery, its deployment can introduce operational complexities that may lead to service disruptions or failed validations. Diagnosing and resolving DNSSEC-related problems demands a deep understanding of the DNSSEC validation chain, as well as familiarity with common misconfigurations and systemic dependencies that impact DNSSEC functionality.

One of the most common DNSSEC troubleshooting scenarios occurs when a resolver reports that a DNS response is bogus, meaning it has failed validation checks. This can stem from various causes, such as expired signatures, incorrect DNSKEY or DS records, mismatched cryptographic hashes, or missing signatures. The first step when addressing bogus responses is to isolate where in the trust chain the validation process is breaking down. Administrators should start by reviewing the RRSIG records in the DNS response and verifying their validity dates. If the RRSIG's expiration date has passed or the inception date is set in the future, the resolver will reject the signature, and the query will fail validation.

Another frequent issue arises when the DS record published in the parent zone does not match the hash of the child zone's KSK. This mismatch disrupts the chain of trust, preventing validating resolvers from confirming the legitimacy of the child zone's DNSKEY. Administrators can use DNS diagnostic tools such as DNSViz to visualize the chain of trust and identify where DS and DNSKEY records diverge. Correcting this issue requires updating the DS record in the parent zone to match the new KSK hash or rolling back the KSK to match the current DS record if the new DS has not yet been published.

Improperly signed zones are another common source of DNSSEC issues. For example, administrators may forget to sign newly added records or may inadvertently remove RRSIG records during manual zone updates. Automated signing tools or inline signing features offered by DNS servers like BIND can help mitigate this risk, but manual intervention still introduces opportunities for oversight. When troubleshooting, administrators should verify that all resource record sets (RRsets) in the zone have corresponding RRSIG records. Missing signatures will prevent validating resolvers from confirming the integrity of the affected RRsets, causing queries for those records to fail validation.

Signature validity periods must also be closely monitored. DNSSEC relies on time-based signature validity to protect against replay attacks, but this also means that expired signatures are treated as invalid. If signature refresh processes are not automated, or if key rollover procedures are delayed, expired RRSIG records will result in resolution failures. Administrators should verify the TTL (Time-To-Live) values of DNS records and ensure that signature refresh intervals are scheduled well in advance of expiration dates. Tools like OpenDNSSEC or BIND's auto-signing features can help automate this process and reduce the risk of human error.

Network infrastructure can also contribute to DNSSEC issues. DNSSEC signatures and additional records such as DNSKEYs and NSEC/NSEC3 records increase the size of DNS responses, sometimes exceeding the 512-byte limit of traditional UDP DNS. If firewalls, load balancers, or other middleboxes block or truncate large DNS responses, queries may fail or resolvers may experience unnecessary TCP fallback, introducing latency. To troubleshoot this, administrators should inspect network devices along the DNS query path to ensure that EDNS0 is enabled and that UDP packets larger than 512 bytes are permitted. Packet captures using tools such as Wireshark can reveal if DNSSEC-related responses are being fragmented or dropped.

It is also common to encounter validation failures due to clock skew between DNS resolvers and authoritative servers. DNSSEC relies on time-based parameters to verify signature validity periods. If a resolver's system clock is out of sync with the authoritative server's clock, it may incorrectly treat valid signatures as expired or not yet valid. Ensuring that all servers involved in DNSSEC operations synchronize with reliable Network Time Protocol (NTP) servers is a simple yet critical step in preventing such discrepancies.

Misconfigured NSEC or NSEC3 records can also cause negative responses to fail validation. NSEC and NSEC3 records provide authenticated denial of existence, proving that a queried name does not exist in the zone. If these records are missing, incorrectly generated, or signed with an invalid key, resolvers will be unable to validate non-existence responses. Troubleshooting this issue involves reviewing the NSEC/NSEC3 chain to ensure that the records correctly cover all unsigned names and that their signatures are valid and within the correct validity window.

Another potential issue is the presence of inconsistent DNSSEC configurations across different authoritative servers in multi-server or geographically distributed deployments. For example, if one authoritative server serves an outdated zone file missing recent DNSSEC signatures, while another serves a correctly signed version, resolvers may receive different responses depending on which server answers the query. To resolve this, administrators must ensure that all authoritative servers are synchronized and that DNSSEC signing and key management procedures are uniformly applied across the entire DNS infrastructure.

Resolvers themselves may also contribute to DNSSEC problems. If a resolver is not DNSSEC-capable or has DNSSEC validation disabled, it will ignore DNSSEC records, leaving the client unprotected. On the other hand, improperly configured resolvers may attempt to validate DNSSEC records but lack an up-to-date trust anchor, resulting in validation failures. Verifying that resolvers are configured with the correct root trust anchor and that RFC 5011 automated trust anchor rollover is functioning properly is essential when troubleshooting DNSSEC validation issues.

Finally, effective troubleshooting requires access to comprehensive logging and diagnostic information. DNSSEC-aware resolvers such as Unbound or BIND can be configured to log validation results, including reasons for failures. Logs indicating signature expiration, key mismatches, or missing trust anchors provide valuable clues during the troubleshooting process. External tools such as dig with the +dnssec flag, DNSSEC Analyzer, and DNSSEC Debugger can assist in diagnosing problems from a client perspective, offering additional insight into where the DNSSEC chain is breaking down.

Successful troubleshooting of DNSSEC issues requires not only technical expertise but also a proactive approach to maintenance and monitoring. Regular audits of DNSSEC configurations, automation of repetitive processes such as re-signing and key rollovers, and clear operational procedures for handling validation failures are all essential components of a resilient DNSSEC deployment. By understanding and addressing the root causes of DNSSEC issues, administrators can ensure that DNSSEC continues to provide the integrity, authenticity, and trust that organizations depend on to secure their DNS infrastructure.

DNSSEC Monitoring and Logging

DNSSEC monitoring and logging are essential components of a secure and reliable DNS infrastructure. While DNSSEC adds cryptographic protection to DNS responses, ensuring authenticity and integrity, maintaining its effectiveness requires constant oversight. Without adequate monitoring and logging, organizations run the risk of undetected misconfigurations, signature expirations, or failures in the DNSSEC validation chain. Continuous visibility into DNSSEC operations allows administrators to detect and respond to issues proactively, maintaining the security and availability of DNS services.

One of the primary objectives of DNSSEC monitoring is to ensure that signatures are valid and timely. Every signed DNS record has a corresponding RRSIG record that includes an inception and expiration timestamp. These timestamps dictate the validity period of the signature. If signatures are not refreshed before they expire, resolvers will begin to treat responses as bogus, leading to resolution failures. Monitoring tools must track the lifecycle of signatures across all zones, issuing alerts well before expiration thresholds are reached. This allows administrators to re-sign zones or troubleshoot automated signing systems before services are disrupted.

In addition to signature expiration, DNSSEC monitoring must validate the entire chain of trust. This includes verifying that DNSKEY records align with the Delegation Signer records published in parent zones. A broken chain of trust occurs when the DS record and the child zone's

KSK no longer match due to an incomplete or failed KSK rollover. Continuous monitoring tools should periodically validate this relationship by resolving zones and tracing the trust chain up to the root. Any discrepancy between the DS record and the child zone's DNSKEY must trigger immediate investigation, as this mismatch prevents external resolvers from validating the domain, resulting in service outages.

Logging is equally critical in DNSSEC deployments. DNSSEC-aware resolvers such as Unbound, BIND, and PowerDNS can be configured to log detailed validation events, including successful and failed validations. These logs provide invaluable insight into the health of the DNSSEC deployment and enable administrators to pinpoint the root cause of validation failures. A common log entry might indicate an expired signature, a missing trust anchor, or a mismatched key. Collecting and analyzing these logs allows organizations to identify patterns or recurring issues, improving long-term operational reliability.

A key consideration when configuring DNSSEC logging is balancing verbosity with operational efficiency. Excessive logging may consume system resources and complicate incident triage, while insufficient logging can obscure critical information needed to investigate problems. Administrators should configure logging to capture meaningful events, such as validation failures, key rollovers, DNSSEC algorithm deprecation warnings, and anomalies in negative responses involving NSEC or NSEC3 records. Logs should also capture events related to trust anchor updates, particularly if RFC 5011 automated trust anchor rollover is in use.

DNSSEC monitoring should also include proactive alerting and integration with broader security operations. Logs and telemetry data from resolvers and authoritative servers can be fed into a Security Information and Event Management (SIEM) platform. This enables the correlation of DNSSEC events with other security data, helping teams detect wider attack patterns such as DNS cache poisoning attempts, resolver manipulation, or insider threats targeting DNS infrastructure. By setting up threshold-based alerts for repeated bogus responses or an unusual volume of validation failures, organizations can respond swiftly to incidents and minimize their impact.

Another important aspect of DNSSEC monitoring is keeping track of key lifecycle events. Key rollovers, especially for the Key Signing Key, require careful coordination and execution. Monitoring tools must verify that new keys are pre-published, that both old and new keys coexist during transitional periods, and that signatures created with new keys are correctly propagated. Any failure during the key rollover process can be catastrophic, breaking DNS resolution for users worldwide. Automated key management tools such as OpenDNSSEC or BIND's inline signing feature typically provide logs and status indicators that should be incorporated into the overall monitoring strategy.

Beyond internal systems, organizations should leverage external monitoring tools to gain an outside-in perspective of DNSSEC performance. Services such as DNSViz, Zonemaster, and Verisign's DNSSEC Debugger allow administrators to analyze public DNS zones and assess how they are perceived by external resolvers. These tools validate trust chains, check for missing or expired signatures, and visualize the DNSSEC hierarchy for specific domains. External monitoring is especially valuable for identifying issues that may only manifest when queries are resolved outside of the organization's internal network.

Network-level monitoring is also relevant to DNSSEC deployments. DNSSEC's larger response sizes, resulting from additional records such as DNSKEY and RRSIG, can lead to transport issues in misconfigured environments. Monitoring should include checks for EDNS0 compliance, ensuring that devices such as firewalls, load balancers, and intrusion detection systems allow large UDP packets and properly handle TCP fallback for DNS traffic. Logs from network devices can reveal packet fragmentation, drops, or anomalies related to DNSSEC-enabled queries, helping to identify bottlenecks or misconfigurations that could affect resolution.

For organizations operating in highly regulated industries, DNSSEC logging and monitoring also support compliance objectives. Regulatory frameworks often require proof of security control effectiveness, and well-maintained DNSSEC logs provide evidence of control operation. Logs documenting successful key rollovers, timely signature refreshes, and the absence of unresolved validation failures contribute to audit readiness and demonstrate that the organization adheres to DNSSEC best practices.

In modern infrastructure, where DNS services may span hybrid and multi-cloud environments, DNSSEC monitoring must be extended to cover all relevant zones and resolvers. Organizations should implement centralized monitoring dashboards that consolidate DNSSEC data across geographically dispersed deployments, providing a unified view of the DNSSEC security posture. In cloud environments, where DNS services may be managed via providers such as AWS Route 53, Azure DNS, or Google Cloud DNS, administrators should take advantage of provider-native monitoring tools to supplement their internal visibility.

An effective DNSSEC monitoring and logging strategy ensures that organizations can detect and respond to DNSSEC issues before they escalate into serious incidents. It enhances operational resilience, maintains the availability of essential services, and protects the trust chain that underpins the secure operation of DNS. By integrating DNSSEC monitoring into broader security and operational processes, organizations can optimize the benefits of DNSSEC and ensure that their DNS infrastructure remains a reliable and secure component of their digital environment.

DNSSEC Performance Considerations

Implementing DNSSEC introduces a range of performance considerations that organizations must address to maintain a secure and responsive DNS infrastructure. While DNSSEC enhances the security of DNS by providing authentication and integrity through digital signatures, it also adds overhead to the traditional DNS resolution process. This additional overhead can affect response sizes, resolver processing times, and network behavior, all of which influence the end-user experience and the efficiency of DNS operations. Understanding the performance impacts of DNSSEC and planning for them effectively is essential for deploying DNSSEC without degrading system performance.

One of the most immediate performance-related concerns with DNSSEC is the increased size of DNS responses. Traditional DNS responses are relatively small, often well within the 512-byte limit for UDP packets. DNSSEC adds several resource record types to the DNS response, such as RRSIG, DNSKEY, NSEC, or NSEC3 records, which significantly increase the size of the response payload. The DNSKEY record alone can add several hundred bytes, and the accompanying RRSIG records further expand the response. When combined with typical resource record sets such as A or AAAA records, the total response size often exceeds the 512-byte UDP limit, requiring the use of the Extension Mechanisms for DNS (EDNS0) to accommodate larger UDP packets.

In environments where EDNS0 is not fully supported by network devices, this increase in response size can lead to DNS response truncation. When this happens, resolvers must fall back to using TCP to complete the DNS transaction, which introduces additional latency due to the TCP handshake and slower transmission of data compared to UDP. Organizations deploying DNSSEC must ensure that firewalls, routers, and middleboxes along the DNS query path support EDNS0 and permit UDP packets larger than 512 bytes, typically up to 4096 bytes, to reduce the likelihood of TCP fallback.

Beyond the transport layer, DNSSEC also impacts the computational load on both authoritative servers and recursive resolvers. On authoritative servers, DNSSEC introduces additional work during zone signing. Every resource record set must be signed with a cryptographic signature using algorithms such as RSA/SHA-256 or ECDSA. Depending on the size of the zone and the number of records, this process can require substantial CPU resources. Although signing generally occurs offline or during scheduled updates, large or frequently updated zones may place a continuous load on servers, particularly if automated signing processes are used.

On the resolver side, DNSSEC validation adds further processing requirements. Resolving a DNSSEC-protected query requires the resolver to perform signature verification for each RRSIG record it encounters. The resolver must also fetch and verify DNSKEY and DS records as it builds the chain of trust from the queried zone to the root. These cryptographic operations, particularly when using RSA-based algorithms, are computationally expensive relative to traditional DNS resolution. In high-traffic environments, this increased processing load can reduce the throughput of recursive resolvers and introduce latency into the resolution process.

To address these performance challenges, organizations can deploy several optimization strategies. The use of more efficient cryptographic algorithms, such as ECDSA P-256, can reduce both the size of DNSSEC signatures and the computational load of validation operations. ECDSA signatures are shorter and faster to verify compared to RSA signatures, which reduces the impact on resolver performance and decreases overall response sizes. However, the choice of algorithm must be balanced against compatibility requirements, as some legacy systems may not fully support newer algorithms.

Caching is another critical factor in mitigating DNSSEC performance impacts. Recursive resolvers typically cache validated DNS responses, including DNSSEC-related records, for the duration of their TTLs. This reduces the frequency with which resolvers must perform full DNSSEC validation for subsequent queries to the same domain. Similarly, caching DNSKEY and DS records higher up in the hierarchy avoids repeatedly querying the parent or root zones for every resolution request. Properly tuning resolver caching parameters can significantly reduce the computational overhead of DNSSEC validation while maintaining a balance between cache freshness and performance.

Load balancing and redundancy also play essential roles in maintaining performance under DNSSEC. Authoritative DNS servers should be distributed geographically and configured in redundant pools to handle increased query loads efficiently. Recursive resolvers performing DNSSEC validation can be scaled horizontally to ensure high availability and distribute processing across multiple nodes. This helps maintain fast response times for end-users, even when DNSSEC-related operations impose higher CPU usage.

In addition to infrastructure optimizations, careful zone management practices contribute to DNSSEC performance. Administrators should minimize unnecessary resource record sets and avoid signing records that do not require DNSSEC protection. For instance, excessive use of wildcards or large zone files containing obsolete records can inflate the number of required signatures, increasing response sizes and validation overhead. Regularly auditing DNS zones and streamlining zone files helps optimize DNSSEC's performance impact.

Monitoring DNSSEC-related performance metrics is crucial for identifying bottlenecks and tuning the DNS environment accordingly. Metrics such as average DNS query resolution time, CPU utilization on recursive resolvers, TCP fallback rates, and DNS packet sizes provide insights into how DNSSEC is affecting system performance. Logging tools and network monitoring platforms can track these metrics in real time, enabling administrators to make data-driven decisions about scaling or optimizing their DNS infrastructure.

Organizations should also consider the potential impact of DNSSEC on distributed denial-of-service (DDoS) resilience. The increased packet sizes associated with DNSSEC can make DNS servers more attractive targets for amplification attacks if they are not properly secured. Rate limiting, response size limits, and filtering of malformed requests are important measures to mitigate such risks while still supporting DNSSEC operations.

Finally, the human factor plays a role in managing DNSSEC performance. Teams responsible for DNSSEC operations must be well-trained in understanding the trade-offs between security and performance. This includes knowledge of DNSSEC tuning parameters, algorithm selection, and best practices for zone design. Collaboration between network engineers, security teams, and system administrators is necessary to align DNSSEC deployment strategies with organizational performance goals.

By addressing these performance considerations early in the DNSSEC planning and implementation process, organizations can achieve a secure and efficient DNS infrastructure that maintains fast, reliable service for users while providing the protection that DNSSEC is designed to offer. Through a combination of technical optimizations, strategic infrastructure investments, and continuous monitoring, the challenges associated with DNSSEC performance can be effectively managed across diverse network environments.

DNSSEC and Recursive Resolvers

Recursive resolvers are a critical component in the DNS ecosystem, acting as intermediaries between end-users and authoritative DNS servers. They receive queries from client devices, resolve domain names by querying multiple authoritative servers, and return the corresponding IP addresses to the clients. When DNSSEC is enabled on a recursive resolver, it performs an additional security function: validating the cryptographic signatures of DNSSEC-protected records to ensure their authenticity and integrity before providing the response to the user. This process, known as DNSSEC validation, transforms the resolver from a simple caching server into a crucial security checkpoint.

When a resolver configured for DNSSEC validation receives a query for a signed domain, it requests not only the traditional DNS records like A or AAAA but also the associated DNSSEC resource records, such as RRSIG and DNSKEY. The resolver uses the DNSKEY records to verify the RRSIG signature applied to the resource record set. If the signature is valid and matches the cryptographic hash of the zone's public key, the resolver knows the data has not been altered in transit. If the resolver cannot validate the signature, it treats the response as bogus and refuses to provide it to the requesting client.

The resolver does not stop validation at the zone level. It also verifies the Delegation Signer record in the parent zone to confirm that the child zone's DNSKEY matches the trusted hash published by the parent. This validation continues up the DNS hierarchy to the root zone, which acts as the trust anchor. Modern recursive resolvers come pre-configured with the root DNSSEC key, which is essential to establishing a complete chain of trust. If this chain is intact, the resolver passes the secure response to the client. If the chain is broken due to an expired signature, a missing record, or a key mismatch, the resolver flags the query as invalid.

Recursive resolvers running DNSSEC validation have a significant role in defending users against attacks like DNS cache poisoning and man-in-the-middle attempts. In cache poisoning, an attacker tries to insert fraudulent data into the resolver's cache. Without DNSSEC, resolvers have no way to verify the authenticity of DNS responses, making it possible for attackers to redirect users to malicious websites. With DNSSEC, however, forged responses will fail signature verification and will not be accepted into the cache, effectively neutralizing this threat.

There are several popular recursive resolvers that support DNSSEC validation, including Unbound, BIND, PowerDNS Recursor, and Knot Resolver. Each of these resolvers can be configured to validate DNSSEC records automatically and reject responses that cannot be validated. Recursive resolvers performing DNSSEC validation are known as validating resolvers, and they provide a higher level of security compared to non-validating alternatives.

While DNSSEC validation significantly improves DNS security, it introduces additional performance considerations for recursive resolvers. Validation requires extra DNS queries to fetch DNSSEC-related records, including DNSKEY and DS records, and it involves cryptographic operations to verify digital signatures. This increases the resolver's CPU usage and the time required to resolve a query. To mitigate the performance impact, recursive resolvers heavily rely on caching. Once a DNSKEY or DS record has been validated and cached, it can be reused for subsequent queries within its TTL, reducing the number of additional lookups and signature verifications needed.

Another factor affecting recursive resolver performance is the handling of DNSSEC response sizes. Signed zones often produce larger DNS responses due to the inclusion of DNSSEC-specific records. If a resolver or the network infrastructure does not support EDNS0 or large UDP packets, it may experience truncated responses that require fallback to TCP, which introduces additional latency. Resolver configurations must be optimized to handle these larger DNSSEC responses efficiently, ensuring that DNS queries do not suffer from unnecessary delays.

Security considerations extend to the management of trust anchors in recursive resolvers. The root DNSSEC key, which serves as the trust anchor for validating responses, is subject to periodic rollover. To facilitate automatic updates of this trust anchor, recursive resolvers implement RFC 5011, a mechanism that allows trust anchors to be updated securely over time. Administrators must ensure that this process is functioning correctly to prevent trust anchor expiration from breaking DNSSEC validation across the entire resolver.

Recursive resolvers must also handle specific edge cases, such as insecure delegations. An insecure delegation occurs when a parent zone does not have a DS record pointing to the child zone's DNSKEY. In such cases, DNSSEC validation stops at the parent zone, and the resolver treats the child zone as unsigned, bypassing further validation for that zone. Understanding how recursive resolvers handle insecure delegations is crucial for troubleshooting and for ensuring that security policies are correctly enforced across all zones.

In multi-resolver deployments, consistency is key. If only some resolvers perform DNSSEC validation while others do not, end-users may experience inconsistent behavior when accessing the same domain. Organizations should ensure that all recursive resolvers in their infrastructure are uniformly configured to validate DNSSEC to prevent confusion and to maintain a unified security posture.

Lastly, recursive resolvers benefit from detailed logging capabilities, allowing administrators to monitor validation outcomes, detect failures, and respond to anomalies. Logs provide insights into signature expiration, trust chain failures, and network issues that may affect DNSSEC validation. Integrating DNSSEC validation logs into centralized monitoring systems enables rapid identification of emerging threats or operational issues related to DNS resolution.

DNSSEC transforms recursive resolvers from passive intermediaries into active guardians of DNS security. By validating the authenticity of DNS responses, recursive resolvers ensure that users only receive trusted data, reducing the risk of DNS-based attacks and supporting the integrity of the broader internet ecosystem. Through careful configuration, performance optimization, and continuous monitoring, recursive resolvers can securely and efficiently deliver DNSSEC-protected data to the clients that depend on them.

DNSSEC and Authoritative Servers

Authoritative DNS servers are responsible for hosting and providing authoritative answers for DNS zones. When DNSSEC is implemented, these servers take on the additional responsibility of serving cryptographically signed DNS data to clients and resolvers. This role is central to the integrity of the DNSSEC framework, as authoritative servers produce the signed records that resolvers later validate to ensure authenticity. Ensuring that authoritative servers are properly configured to support DNSSEC is essential for protecting domains against DNS spoofing, cache poisoning, and data tampering attacks.

The first DNSSEC-related task performed by authoritative servers is publishing DNSKEY records for each signed zone. These records contain the public keys that resolvers use to verify signatures on the resource record sets. The authoritative server must also provide the associated RRSIG records, which include the cryptographic signatures generated by the Zone Signing Key or Key Signing Key. Each resource record set in the zone, such as A, AAAA, MX, or TXT records, must have a corresponding RRSIG record. These signatures are generated by signing the RRsets using private keys, which must be securely stored and carefully managed by administrators.

Authoritative servers also play a key role in providing authenticated denial of existence through NSEC or NSEC3 records. When a resolver queries for a non-existent domain or record, the authoritative server responds with either an NSEC or NSEC3 record that proves the record does not exist. This is essential to prevent attackers from forging negative responses or redirecting traffic to unauthorized destinations. These NSEC or NSEC3 records are also signed with RRSIGs, ensuring that even denials of existence are verifiable through DNSSEC.

The zone signing process is typically automated on authoritative servers using DNSSEC management tools. For instance, BIND offers an inline signing feature that automatically signs new records as they are added to the zone file. Other tools, such as OpenDNSSEC, handle key management and zone signing for authoritative servers, reducing the administrative burden and ensuring that signatures are refreshed before expiration. Automation is particularly important for large or dynamic zones that undergo frequent updates, as manual signing processes are error-prone and unsustainable at scale.

One operational consideration for authoritative servers is managing key rollovers. Regularly rotating the Zone Signing Key and Key Signing

Key is critical to maintaining DNSSEC security. During a key rollover, authoritative servers must publish both the old and new keys in the DNSKEY record set, sign records with the new key, and ensure that resolvers can validate responses using either key until old keys are retired. Additionally, Key Signing Key rollovers require coordination with the parent zone to update the DS record, ensuring that the chain of trust remains unbroken.

Authoritative servers must also accommodate the increased response sizes caused by DNSSEC. The addition of DNSKEY, RRSIG, and NSEC/NSEC3 records significantly enlarges DNS responses. Servers must support EDNS0 to enable responses larger than 512 bytes over UDP and be configured to handle fallback to TCP when necessary. Failure to properly configure servers or network devices to handle these larger DNSSEC responses can result in query truncation and resolution failures.

Security is paramount on authoritative servers operating with DNSSEC. The private keys used to sign zones must be protected using strong access controls and, when possible, stored within secure hardware modules such as Hardware Security Modules (HSMs). Unauthorized access to these keys could allow attackers to forge signatures and compromise the security guarantees of DNSSEC.

Additionally, authoritative servers must be configured to publish all required DNSSEC records consistently across all name servers. Discrepancies between primary and secondary servers, such as missing RRSIG records or outdated key material, can lead to inconsistent responses and validation failures for end-users. Synchronizing zone data and signatures across all authoritative servers is crucial for maintaining the reliability of the DNSSEC deployment.

Authoritative servers also benefit from comprehensive monitoring and logging. Logs should capture events related to zone signing, key rollovers, signature expiration, and anomalies in response behavior. Monitoring systems should track signature freshness and DNSKEY status to ensure that all zones remain compliant with DNSSEC best practices. Alerts for missing or expired signatures allow administrators to resolve issues before they affect DNS resolution for users.

By securely managing keys, automating zone signing, and optimizing server configurations for DNSSEC operations, authoritative servers play a pivotal role in enforcing the authenticity and integrity of DNS data. Their ability to serve trusted, verifiable responses underpins the effectiveness of DNSSEC and helps maintain a secure and resilient global DNS infrastructure.

Case Study: DNSSEC in Government Networks

Government networks are among the most targeted infrastructures in the world due to the critical information and services they manage. From public sector web portals to inter-agency communication platforms and citizen-facing services, government networks rely heavily on DNS to ensure the availability and integrity of their online operations. Recognizing the increasing risk of cyberattacks aimed at DNS vulnerabilities, many national and regional governments have mandated the deployment of DNSSEC across their networks to provide stronger assurance of the authenticity and integrity of DNS responses. One prominent case study involves the deployment of DNSSEC across a national government's core internet and internal DNS infrastructure, with the goal of protecting sensitive services and data from tampering and redirection attacks.

The government in this case study operates a complex network infrastructure comprising several ministries, regulatory agencies, and public service organizations. Each of these entities maintains its own set of domain names, including domains for websites, email servers, internal applications, and secure portals used for citizen services such as tax filing, healthcare access, and voting registration. Given the high stakes involved in maintaining the integrity of these services, the government identified DNSSEC as a foundational component of its cybersecurity modernization initiative.

The first step in the project involved securing the government's authoritative DNS servers. These servers were responsible for hosting the zones of all the official domains under the government's top-level domain. The project team implemented DNSSEC by generating and managing Zone Signing Keys and Key Signing Keys for each zone, ensuring that every resource record set was signed and accompanied by RRSIG records. Special attention was paid to sensitive domains, such as those handling legal documents, citizen identification records, and government-to-government communication platforms, as these domains were considered high-priority targets for attackers.

To establish a valid chain of trust, the project team coordinated with the national top-level domain registry to submit and publish DS records for each signed zone. This step was critical to ensuring that external resolvers could validate the authenticity of DNS responses served by the government's authoritative servers. By linking each zone's KSK to the parent zone through DS records, the team ensured that any external DNS resolver capable of DNSSEC validation could trust responses received from the government's domains.

The deployment was accompanied by a significant effort to modernize internal DNS infrastructure. The government's internal networks relied heavily on recursive resolvers to handle DNS queries for users located in ministry offices, government agencies, and secure facilities. These resolvers were upgraded to fully support DNSSEC validation. Every DNS response, whether for internal domains or external internet resources, was subject to cryptographic validation before being provided to end-users. This measure provided an additional layer of protection for government employees and systems, preventing forged DNS responses from redirecting traffic to malicious websites or fake internal services.

In addition to external DNS zones, internal domains were also signed with DNSSEC. This move was crucial in securing the internal communication channels between government agencies. Sensitive services, such as internal file-sharing platforms, secure messaging applications, and document management systems, depended on internal DNS to resolve hostnames to IP addresses. By signing internal zones and enforcing DNSSEC validation internally, the government reduced the risk of insider threats and mitigated the impact of potential supply chain attacks on internal networks.

As part of the DNSSEC deployment, the government implemented an automated key management system to handle ZSK rollovers and re-signing operations. Due to the high number of zones involved and the critical nature of the services they supported, automation was vital to prevent human errors that could lead to expired signatures or broken validation chains. Regular audits and monitoring were introduced to track the health of DNSSEC signatures, key expiration dates, and the integrity of the trust chain. Automated alerts were configured to notify network operations teams of any anomalies or potential issues requiring immediate attention.

The deployment also extended to government-contracted service providers. Any third-party vendor managing domains or hosting services on behalf of government agencies was required to implement DNSSEC as a contractual obligation. This measure ensured that the government's DNSSEC policy was consistently applied across the entire digital supply chain, reducing the risk of exposure through externally managed domains.

Throughout the deployment, the government placed a strong emphasis on staff training and cross-agency collaboration. Network administrators, security personnel, and IT teams from each agency participated in workshops and tabletop exercises to build expertise in DNSSEC operations, troubleshooting, and incident response. This collaborative approach helped foster a unified understanding of DNSSEC's importance across the public sector, ensuring that all agencies remained aligned with the national cybersecurity strategy.

One of the key challenges faced during implementation was ensuring that legacy systems and applications remained compatible with DNSSEC-enabled services. Some internal applications had hardcoded DNS resolvers or were developed without consideration for DNSSEC. To address this, the government conducted a thorough assessment of legacy systems and, where necessary, upgraded or modified applications to ensure they could handle larger DNS responses and properly interact with DNSSEC-validating resolvers.

Following the successful implementation of DNSSEC, the government observed tangible security improvements. Security operations centers reported a significant reduction in successful DNS-based attacks and phishing attempts that relied on DNS manipulation. Additionally, public trust in citizen-facing services, such as online voting registration and tax filing systems, was strengthened by the knowledge that these services were now protected by DNSSEC, making them resistant to redirection and data interception.

The case study highlights the critical role DNSSEC plays in protecting high-value domains and services within government networks. By securing both external and internal DNS infrastructure, the government created a more resilient digital environment capable of defending against modern cyber threats targeting the DNS layer. The success of this deployment served as a model for other public sector organizations, inspiring additional initiatives to adopt DNSSEC in other sectors, including healthcare, law enforcement, and education. Through continued investment in DNSSEC and complementary security measures, the government laid the foundation for a more secure and trustworthy public sector digital ecosystem.

Case Study: DNSSEC in Financial Institutions

The financial sector is one of the most heavily targeted industries by cybercriminals due to the nature of its services and the sensitive data it handles. Financial institutions, including banks, investment firms, payment processors, and credit unions, face constant threats from attackers attempting to manipulate DNS traffic to intercept transactions, harvest customer credentials, or redirect users to fraudulent websites. In response to these risks, many financial institutions have implemented DNSSEC as part of a broader effort to protect their DNS infrastructure from tampering and to safeguard customer trust. This case study explores the deployment of DNSSEC within a large multinational bank and the operational and security benefits it provided.

The bank in question operates hundreds of domains for its public websites, online banking platforms, trading portals, APIs, and internal networks spanning multiple regions. Given its global footprint and reputation as a trusted financial services provider, the bank's leadership recognized that DNS vulnerabilities posed a significant risk not only to customer transactions but also to brand reputation and regulatory compliance. Executives and security officers determined that DNSSEC implementation was a necessary step to reinforce the integrity of DNS queries and protect against DNS-based attacks, such as cache poisoning and domain hijacking.

The deployment project began with a comprehensive audit of all external domains under the bank's control. These included domains used for customer-facing services like online banking, corporate websites, mobile banking applications, secure messaging platforms, and business-to-business payment services. Each of these domains was classified according to its business criticality and exposure risk. High-value domains, such as the bank's primary online banking portal and API endpoints used for partner integrations, were prioritized for immediate DNSSEC deployment.

The first phase involved DNSSEC signing of the external zones managed by the bank's authoritative DNS servers. The IT security team implemented a dual-key model by generating both Zone Signing Keys and Key Signing Keys for each zone. DNSKEY records and corresponding RRSIG records were created and published in the DNS. Each domain's KSK was then securely submitted to the parent registry for DS record publication, establishing the trust anchor necessary for resolvers to validate the authenticity of responses.

Because the bank operated across multiple jurisdictions, it had to coordinate with several domain registrars and national domain registries to ensure that DS records were correctly handled and propagated. In some regions, where registrars lacked automation for DNSSEC, the bank's DNS administrators manually submitted DS records and maintained detailed records to track each delegation's status. The project emphasized end-to-end validation testing at every stage, using external tools to verify that the trust chain was intact and that resolvers could validate DNS responses from the bank's domains without issues.

To protect internal systems, the bank extended DNSSEC to internal zones used across its corporate offices, data centers, and secure transaction networks. Recursive resolvers located in internal networks were configured to enforce DNSSEC validation on all queries. This measure ensured that internal services, such as employee portals, secure file-sharing platforms, and corporate authentication systems, were protected from DNS tampering and man-in-the-middle attacks.

The bank's DNSSEC deployment was tightly integrated with its broader cybersecurity strategy, which included multi-factor authentication, Transport Layer Security (TLS) for web and API traffic, and secure email protocols such as DMARC, DKIM, and SPF. DNSSEC complemented these controls by protecting the DNS layer, which underpins every connection initiated by the bank's employees, partners, and customers.

To address the risk of key compromise or expiration, the bank implemented an automated key management system that handled periodic ZSK rollovers and re-signing operations. The KSK rollovers were carefully planned, with the IT security team coordinating with the domain registries well in advance to ensure a seamless transition. Automated alerting was configured to notify administrators of impending key expirations, signing errors, or anomalies in the trust chain.

As a highly regulated entity, the bank was subject to stringent requirements under national and international financial regulations. DNSSEC deployment was aligned with regulatory obligations to ensure the confidentiality, integrity, and availability of financial data and services. During regulatory audits, the bank provided documentation demonstrating that DNSSEC was implemented on all critical domains, supported by validation logs showing consistent and successful DNSSEC checks.

One of the key benefits observed after DNSSEC deployment was a reduction in phishing campaigns that leveraged lookalike or compromised domains. By protecting its domains with DNSSEC, the bank made it significantly harder for attackers to poison DNS caches or redirect customers to fake login pages masquerading as the bank's legitimate website. While DNSSEC did not prevent phishing outright, it strengthened the bank's defense against DNS-level manipulation that could have enabled such attacks.

The deployment also improved trust in the bank's API ecosystem. The bank maintained partnerships with fintech firms, payment processors, and institutional clients who relied on API integrations for payment processing and data exchange. These partners, often operating their own DNSSEC-validating resolvers, benefited from the added assurance that responses from the bank's API domains could be authenticated, reducing the likelihood of API traffic being redirected or intercepted.

One of the challenges encountered during deployment was ensuring that legacy systems, particularly older network appliances and custom applications, were compatible with DNSSEC's larger DNS response sizes. Some appliances and services had limitations on UDP payload sizes or lacked EDNS0 support, leading to issues with truncated responses. The bank's IT team mitigated this by upgrading affected systems and reconfiguring network devices to properly handle EDNS0 and fallback to TCP where necessary.

Training and awareness played a critical role in the project's success. The bank's technical teams, including DNS administrators, security engineers, and network operations staff, underwent DNSSEC-specific training to build the skills required for day-to-day management and incident response. A dedicated DNSSEC monitoring platform was integrated into the bank's SIEM system, providing real-time alerts on DNSSEC validation anomalies, expired signatures, and resolver-related incidents.

After completing the deployment, the bank conducted quarterly DNSSEC audits to verify compliance with internal security policies and regulatory requirements. These audits involved reviewing key management practices, analyzing resolver logs, validating DS records in the parent zones, and simulating incident response scenarios related to DNSSEC failures. The proactive approach ensured that DNSSEC remained an effective and well-maintained security control within the bank's overall infrastructure.

The case study highlights how DNSSEC strengthens trust in financial services by securing the foundational DNS infrastructure that supports customer transactions, partner integrations, and internal operations. By eliminating vulnerabilities at the DNS layer, the bank reduced its exposure to DNS-based attacks and improved customer confidence in its online platforms, reinforcing its position as a security-conscious leader in the financial sector.

DNSSEC Adoption Worldwide

The adoption of DNSSEC worldwide has followed a complex and uneven trajectory, shaped by a combination of technical, regulatory, economic, and organizational factors. While the Domain Name System Security Extensions were introduced to address well-known vulnerabilities in the global DNS infrastructure, the pace of DNSSEC implementation has varied significantly across regions, industries, and types of organizations. Some countries and sectors have led the way in DNSSEC deployment, setting benchmarks for security and resilience, while others have lagged due to concerns over operational complexity, cost, or perceived necessity.

One of the earliest and most impactful milestones in global DNSSEC adoption occurred in July 2010, when the DNS root zone was signed, creating the foundation for a hierarchical chain of trust across the global DNS system. This pivotal event enabled top-level domain operators and second-level domain owners to link their DNS zones to the root through DS records, allowing resolvers to validate responses from their domains cryptographically. Since then, many top-level domains (TLDs), including both generic TLDs such as .com, .org, and .net, as well as numerous country-code TLDs like .se, .nl, and .cz, have deployed DNSSEC and offered DNSSEC support to registrants.

Northern and Western Europe have been particularly strong proponents of DNSSEC. Countries like Sweden and the Netherlands were among the first to adopt DNSSEC at a national level, with Sweden's .se TLD signing its zone as early as 2005. These countries not only implemented DNSSEC within their registries but also fostered widespread adoption among domain registrants, supported by government initiatives and industry partnerships. The Dutch government, for example, has mandated DNSSEC for certain government services and has worked alongside the private sector to encourage its uptake in the broader business community.

In the United States, DNSSEC deployment has been driven in part by federal mandates. The Office of Management and Budget (OMB) issued directives requiring all federal agencies to implement DNSSEC on their external-facing domains. This initiative resulted in the widespread deployment of DNSSEC across .gov domains, protecting a variety of government services, including tax systems, military platforms, and citizen engagement portals. Beyond the public sector, adoption in the private sector has been more gradual, with financial institutions and technology companies leading the charge due to their heightened sensitivity to DNS-based threats.

Asia-Pacific countries have demonstrated a mixed level of DNSSEC adoption. Some national registries, such as Japan's .jp and South Korea's .kr, have enabled DNSSEC signing for their domains and encouraged adoption among registrants. However, many other ccTLDs in the region have been slower to implement DNSSEC, reflecting broader variations in cybersecurity maturity and regulatory enforcement. Despite this uneven deployment, awareness of DNSSEC's benefits has grown steadily, particularly in nations that have experienced high-profile DNS-based cyber incidents.

In Latin America and the Caribbean, adoption has progressed as part of broader internet security and resilience programs. Organizations such as LACNIC, the regional internet registry, have promoted DNSSEC through capacity-building workshops, training, and advocacy. Countries like Brazil and Argentina have taken proactive steps to encourage DNSSEC adoption, although deployment levels among registrants remain modest compared to regions like Europe. One of the common challenges in the region has been the limited availability of technical expertise and resources to manage DNSSEC operations, especially among smaller registrars and domain owners.

Africa's DNSSEC adoption landscape is still emerging. Several African ccTLDs, such as .za (South Africa) and .ke (Kenya), have signed their zones and offer DNSSEC services, but adoption at the domain holder level is relatively low. Efforts by organizations like AFRINIC and ISOC to promote DNSSEC awareness and training have laid the groundwork for further expansion. Nevertheless, infrastructure constraints and limited access to skilled personnel continue to impede widespread deployment in many African countries.

Globally, the commercial sector's adoption of DNSSEC has been driven by high-risk industries, including finance, healthcare, and e-commerce. Companies operating in these sectors face strict data protection and regulatory requirements, making DNSSEC a valuable addition to their security frameworks. Online retailers, financial service providers, and cloud service platforms increasingly view DNSSEC as essential to safeguarding customer interactions, protecting APIs, and defending against DNS hijacking and cache poisoning attacks.

Despite these advancements, global DNSSEC adoption still faces hurdles. One of the most cited challenges is the perceived complexity of DNSSEC deployment and management. Many organizations, especially smaller enterprises, lack the in-house expertise to handle key generation, rollover processes, zone signing, and DS record submission. Others express concerns about potential performance impacts, such as larger DNS responses leading to issues with legacy systems or network devices.

Another barrier is a lack of incentives from domain registrars. While most major registrars now support DNSSEC, not all actively promote it or offer automated tools to simplify deployment for customers. In some cases, DNSSEC signing is offered as a premium service, creating a financial disincentive for smaller organizations or personal website owners to adopt it.

Public perception and demand also play a role. End-users typically remain unaware of DNSSEC, and there is limited pressure from consumers for businesses to implement it. Unlike the visible security indicators associated with HTTPS, DNSSEC operates behind the scenes, providing protection at the infrastructure level but offering no direct user interface or notification to visitors. As a result, organizations may prioritize other security initiatives that deliver more immediately recognizable benefits to customers.

Nonetheless, DNSSEC adoption continues to expand gradually. Initiatives from global organizations such as ICANN, IETF, and ISOC, as well as regional internet registries and national governments, are helping raise awareness and promote best practices. Increasing integration of DNSSEC into cloud-based DNS services, such as those offered by AWS Route 53, Google Cloud DNS, and Azure DNS, has also made it easier for businesses to deploy DNSSEC without managing the underlying infrastructure themselves.

As DNSSEC adoption grows, it strengthens the overall security and stability of the internet. Each signed zone contributes to building a more trustworthy global DNS environment where attackers find it increasingly difficult to manipulate DNS records and redirect traffic for malicious purposes. While the journey toward universal DNSSEC deployment is ongoing, the steady progress made across different regions and sectors underscores a global recognition of the importance of securing the DNS layer as a fundamental part of modern internet infrastructure.

DNSSEC and Emerging Technologies

As emerging technologies continue to reshape the digital landscape, the role of DNSSEC has expanded beyond its traditional place in securing DNS queries. Modern innovations such as 5G, Internet of Things (IoT), edge computing, blockchain, and zero trust architectures are all heavily reliant on robust, secure, and resilient DNS infrastructure. The deployment of DNSSEC is becoming increasingly intertwined with these technologies, supporting their security requirements and helping to prevent evolving threats that target the DNS layer. The interplay between DNSSEC and emerging technologies is crucial in reinforcing the security posture of next-generation networks and services.

With the global rollout of 5G networks, service providers are under increasing pressure to secure the massive surge in devices, connections, and data transactions facilitated by ultra-low latency and high-bandwidth networks. 5G networks rely on DNS for resolving domain names to support critical functions such as mobile edge computing (MEC), network slicing, and device authentication. Given that DNS traffic within 5G architectures may traverse public and private domains, the integrity and authenticity of DNS responses become paramount. DNSSEC helps secure 5G DNS queries by protecting them from tampering and spoofing, ensuring that network slices and mobile applications resolve only to authorized endpoints. This is particularly important as 5G supports industries like autonomous vehicles, smart manufacturing, and critical infrastructure, where DNS manipulation could have dire consequences.

In the IoT space, DNSSEC plays an equally important role. IoT ecosystems comprise millions of interconnected devices that often depend on DNS to communicate with cloud services, controllers, and other IoT devices. As these devices are typically resource-constrained, they are more vulnerable to DNS-related attacks, such as cache poisoning or rogue firmware distribution through DNS redirection. By integrating DNSSEC validation into IoT networks, either directly within more capable devices or via DNSSEC-validating recursive resolvers, organizations can protect device communications and mitigate risks associated with DNS forgery. This is critical in sectors such as smart cities, healthcare, and industrial control systems, where secure DNS resolution can help prevent large-scale disruptions or physical harm.

Edge computing is another rapidly growing technology that relies heavily on secure and efficient DNS. Edge computing moves computation and storage closer to the end-users to reduce latency and bandwidth usage. Edge nodes and devices frequently communicate with each other and with cloud backends using DNS. As workloads are increasingly distributed to the network edge, ensuring the authenticity of DNS resolutions is key to maintaining secure communications. DNSSEC contributes to edge computing environments by preventing malicious actors from redirecting traffic from edge devices to rogue or unauthorized services. This is especially valuable in distributed deployments where centralized oversight is reduced, and edge nodes may be deployed in less physically secure environments.

Blockchain and distributed ledger technologies have also introduced innovative models for trust and decentralization, yet even these systems are not immune to DNS-related risks. While blockchain-based systems often operate on decentralized principles, they still rely on traditional DNS infrastructure for accessing user interfaces, APIs, and off-chain services. A compromised DNS record could misdirect blockchain users to fraudulent websites, compromising wallets, smart contracts, or other sensitive assets. DNSSEC helps mitigate this risk by ensuring that DNS responses involved in blockchain ecosystem interactions, such as visiting a decentralized finance (DeFi) platform's web portal or API gateway, are authenticated and unaltered.

Additionally, emerging technologies such as secure multi-party computation (MPC), confidential computing, and federated learning increasingly depend on reliable DNS for establishing secure channels between distributed parties and nodes. DNSSEC supports these models by ensuring that the endpoints involved in secure computations or collaborative AI training resolve to legitimate servers and are not hijacked through DNS manipulation.

Zero trust architectures, which have gained traction as a modern cybersecurity framework, emphasize the principle that no system or user should be automatically trusted, whether inside or outside the network perimeter. DNSSEC aligns with the zero trust model by addressing DNS vulnerabilities that could otherwise serve as a trust loophole. In a zero trust environment, DNSSEC ensures that every DNS resolution is cryptographically validated before establishing a connection, complementing identity verification, micro-segmentation, and continuous monitoring strategies.

The growing trend of Software-Defined Networking (SDN) and Network Functions Virtualization (NFV) in modern data centers and telecom networks also highlights the relevance of DNSSEC. Virtualized network functions and dynamic routing decisions within SDN environments often depend on DNS to direct traffic flows, instantiate virtual services, and connect distributed components. DNSSEC provides the underlying DNS security necessary to protect these processes from interference by attackers seeking to disrupt network operations or reroute traffic for eavesdropping or denial of service purposes.

As artificial intelligence (AI) and machine learning (ML) technologies continue to automate and optimize network operations and cybersecurity defense mechanisms, DNSSEC plays an increasingly foundational role in supplying accurate data. AI-driven security solutions often analyze DNS logs to detect anomalies, identify command and control traffic, or recognize phishing campaigns. The integrity of this data is critical. DNSSEC helps ensure that the DNS telemetry feeding these AI models is trustworthy and free from forged records, improving the effectiveness of machine learning-based threat detection and network forensics.

In cloud-native environments, Kubernetes and container orchestration platforms rely on internal DNS services to resolve service names to dynamic IP addresses within clusters. DNSSEC enhances security within these environments by validating DNS responses between services and microservices, reducing the risk of internal DNS spoofing or unauthorized service redirection. This ensures the integrity of service discovery in cloud-native applications and protects inter-service communication in microservices architectures.

DNSSEC's role will only grow as quantum computing emerges on the horizon. Quantum computers could eventually break many of the cryptographic algorithms currently used in DNSSEC, such as RSA. However, efforts are already underway to prepare DNSSEC for a post-quantum world by exploring quantum-resistant algorithms. The integration of these algorithms into DNSSEC will be vital in ensuring that DNS security remains effective against future quantum-enabled attacks.

As the digital ecosystem becomes increasingly reliant on automation, decentralization, and distributed computing models, the need for secure, verifiable DNS becomes more pressing. DNSSEC's ability to safeguard DNS queries makes it a crucial component in the security frameworks of these emerging technologies, reinforcing trust in communications and service availability across next-generation networks and infrastructures. Organizations that embrace emerging technologies must consider DNSSEC as a foundational layer of protection to mitigate the DNS-related risks inherent in these new paradigms.

DNSSEC Interoperability Challenges

DNSSEC, while providing an essential layer of security for the Domain Name System, has faced several interoperability challenges that have affected its widespread adoption and seamless integration across diverse environments. These challenges arise from the variety of DNS implementations, resolver behaviors, registrar policies, and network configurations present across the global internet. Each component of the DNS ecosystem, from authoritative servers to recursive resolvers to registrars, must correctly implement and support DNSSEC for its benefits to be fully realized. However, inconsistencies and limitations at these points often introduce operational difficulties and prevent DNSSEC from functioning smoothly across all systems.

One significant interoperability issue involves the varying levels of DNSSEC support among registrars and domain registries. While most major top-level domains now support DNSSEC, not all registrars provide streamlined mechanisms for customers to submit and manage Delegation Signer (DS) records. In many cases, domain owners are required to manually generate and transmit DS records to their registrar through non-standardized or cumbersome interfaces. Some registrars still lack automation capabilities, forcing customers to depend on manual workflows that can lead to errors or delays in establishing the DNSSEC chain of trust. This inconsistency complicates DNSSEC deployment, especially for organizations managing large numbers of domains across different registrars and TLDs.

Differences in resolver behavior present another common interoperability challenge. Recursive resolvers vary in how strictly they enforce DNSSEC validation policies, handle fallback scenarios, and interpret edge cases such as unsigned zones or insecure delegations. For example, while one resolver may strictly enforce DNSSEC validation and reject improperly signed responses, another may be configured to allow unsigned responses or selectively disable DNSSEC validation under specific conditions. This lack of uniformity can result in inconsistent resolution experiences, where some users receive valid responses while others encounter resolution failures depending on the resolver path. The inconsistency across resolvers is particularly problematic for large organizations that rely on both internal and external resolvers in hybrid environments.

Network infrastructure limitations can also affect DNSSEC interoperability. DNSSEC increases the size of DNS responses due to the inclusion of additional resource records such as RRSIG, DNSKEY, and NSEC/NSEC3 records. Many legacy firewalls, load balancers, and middleboxes are configured to block or truncate DNS packets exceeding the traditional 512-byte UDP limit. While EDNS0 extensions allow for larger UDP payloads, not all network devices are correctly configured to handle EDNS0-enabled packets. Inconsistent EDNS0 support along the query path may force resolvers to fall back to TCP unnecessarily, adding latency or causing resolution timeouts if TCP is blocked or restricted. These issues can lead to intermittent DNS failures that are difficult to diagnose, particularly in networks with complex routing and security policies.

The choice of cryptographic algorithms also introduces interoperability concerns. While DNSSEC initially relied on algorithms such as RSA/SHA-1 and RSA/SHA-256, newer algorithms like ECDSA P-256 are gaining adoption due to their smaller key sizes and faster signature validation. However, not all resolvers or DNS infrastructure components fully support the newer algorithms, particularly in environments where older or proprietary DNS software is still in use. Domain owners who adopt modern algorithms to reduce response sizes and improve performance may inadvertently encounter compatibility issues with legacy systems that cannot validate signatures using these newer cryptographic methods.

Another challenge arises with internationalized domain names (IDNs). IDNs, which allow non-ASCII characters in domain names through punycode encoding, require careful handling when combined with DNSSEC. Both authoritative servers and resolvers must correctly interpret and sign IDNs according to the same canonicalization rules. Inconsistent handling of IDNs, including variations in how different DNS software processes punycode conversions, can result in signature verification failures. This is particularly relevant for global businesses or governments that serve diverse linguistic communities and depend on IDNs for local or regional branding.

In addition to technical issues, policy and governance differences across organizations contribute to DNSSEC interoperability gaps. Some organizations may enforce strict internal DNSSEC policies that mandate validation for all zones, while others may adopt a more relaxed stance, particularly when dealing with legacy systems that cannot support DNSSEC. The result is a fragmented DNSSEC deployment landscape, where end-to-end trust is difficult to guarantee. Organizations participating in cross-border collaborations or supply chains may find that their DNSSEC policies are not consistently mirrored by their partners, leaving parts of their DNS infrastructure vulnerable.

DNSSEC's interaction with other DNS-based security protocols introduces further interoperability complexities. Protocols such as DANE (DNS-Based Authentication of Named Entities) depend on DNSSEC to validate TLSA records used for authenticating TLS sessions. If DNSSEC is inconsistently applied across domains or between parent and child zones, DANE validation may fail even when the TLSA records are correctly configured. Similarly, DNSSEC works alongside SPF, DKIM, and DMARC to secure email systems. If DNS records for these protocols are improperly signed or fail DNSSEC validation due to interoperability issues, email delivery and authentication may be disrupted.

Interoperability challenges also affect monitoring and troubleshooting processes. Administrators depend on diagnostic tools such as dig, DNSViz, and DNSSEC Debugger to analyze DNSSEC configurations and identify trust chain issues. However, variations in how different tools parse and interpret DNSSEC data can lead to inconsistent results. Moreover, differences in log formats and diagnostic output from DNS servers and resolvers complicate efforts to correlate data and quickly resolve issues. A lack of standardization in DNSSEC diagnostic practices contributes to delayed incident response and greater operational overhead.

Efforts to improve DNSSEC interoperability are ongoing. The Internet Engineering Task Force (IETF) regularly publishes updates to DNSSEC-related RFCs to clarify specifications, address known issues, and encourage best practices. Industry groups, such as the DNS Operations, Analysis, and Research Center (DNS-OARC), promote collaboration among operators to address operational challenges. However, progress remains uneven, as adoption depends on individual organizations, infrastructure providers, and software vendors committing to fully supporting and updating their systems.

Ultimately, addressing DNSSEC interoperability challenges requires a combination of technical upgrades, organizational cooperation, and industry-wide alignment on standards and best practices. As DNSSEC continues to play a vital role in securing global DNS infrastructure, resolving these challenges will be crucial to ensuring a reliable, secure, and universally trusted DNS ecosystem. Organizations adopting DNSSEC must plan for compatibility testing, network validation, and cross-vendor integration to overcome these barriers and achieve a seamless deployment experience.

DNSSEC and Quantum Computing

The intersection of DNSSEC and quantum computing represents a crucial area of focus for the future of internet security. DNSSEC was designed to secure the Domain Name System by providing cryptographic assurance of the authenticity and integrity of DNS responses. However, the emergence of quantum computing threatens to undermine the cryptographic algorithms upon which DNSSEC currently relies. As quantum computing advances from theoretical research to practical application, it is imperative to assess the impact it will have on DNSSEC and to plan for the evolution of the protocol in a post-quantum world.

DNSSEC relies heavily on public key cryptography to secure DNS zones and validate signatures. The most widely used algorithms in DNSSEC deployments today are RSA with SHA-256 and elliptic curve algorithms like ECDSA P-256. These algorithms are considered secure against classical computers due to the computational infeasibility of breaking them using conventional factoring or discrete logarithm methods. However, quantum computers, when fully realized, will have the capability to execute Shor's algorithm, a quantum algorithm that can efficiently factor large integers and solve discrete logarithm problems. This means that algorithms like RSA and ECDSA, which form the cryptographic backbone of DNSSEC, could be rendered obsolete by sufficiently powerful quantum systems.

If a quantum computer were able to break RSA or ECDSA, an attacker could forge RRSIG records by deriving the private key from a publicly available DNSKEY record. This would allow malicious actors to craft fraudulent DNS responses that would pass validation checks at recursive resolvers, effectively bypassing the DNSSEC protections designed to prevent cache poisoning and DNS hijacking. The global trust in DNSSEC would be compromised, and the integrity of critical internet services relying on DNSSEC could be put at risk.

In anticipation of these threats, the cryptography and DNS communities have begun to explore quantum-resistant, or post-quantum, cryptographic algorithms suitable for DNSSEC. The National Institute of Standards and Technology (NIST) has been leading efforts to standardize post-quantum cryptographic algorithms through its Post-Quantum Cryptography (PQC) project. The goal is to identify algorithms that can resist quantum attacks while remaining efficient and practical for real-world applications, including DNSSEC.

One of the key challenges in integrating post-quantum cryptography into DNSSEC is the need to balance security with performance and efficiency. DNS responses are subject to size limitations, especially when transported over UDP. DNSSEC already increases response sizes due to the inclusion of RRSIG, DNSKEY, and other related records. Many candidate post-quantum algorithms, such as lattice-based schemes, produce significantly larger public keys and signatures than traditional algorithms like RSA or ECDSA. This creates additional stress on DNS transport mechanisms, including EDNS0-enabled responses and fallback to TCP, and could lead to increased latency or higher failure rates in constrained network environments.

Despite these challenges, the DNS community is actively researching potential post-quantum algorithms that could feasibly integrate into DNSSEC without severely degrading performance. Algorithms under consideration include CRYSTALS-Dilithium and FALCON, both of which have been selected by NIST as finalists in its PQC standardization process. These algorithms promise to offer resistance to quantum attacks while keeping key and signature sizes within an acceptable range for DNS applications. However, adopting such algorithms at scale will require extensive testing, software updates, and cooperation among DNS server vendors, resolver operators, registrars, and domain owners.

The introduction of quantum-resistant algorithms into DNSSEC will also necessitate updates to existing RFCs and the creation of new operational standards. This will include defining new DNSSEC record types, such as additional DNSKEY and RRSIG variants that accommodate post-quantum signatures. Careful planning will be needed to facilitate smooth transitions, including dual-algorithm strategies where both classical and quantum-resistant signatures coexist in zones during the migration period. This will allow resolvers that support post-quantum algorithms to validate the new records while maintaining backward compatibility with existing systems that only recognize traditional cryptographic methods.

Beyond technical considerations, the DNSSEC and quantum computing intersection raises important policy and governance questions. Key internet governance bodies, such as ICANN, the IETF, and national cybersecurity agencies, will play a critical role in shaping global consensus on when and how to begin migrating DNSSEC to quantum-safe algorithms. Given the scale and complexity of the internet's DNS infrastructure, transitioning to post-quantum cryptography will be a multi-year effort requiring coordinated action across both public and private sectors.

Another consideration is the timeline for quantum computing development. While quantum computers capable of breaking RSA-2048 and similar algorithms do not yet exist, advances in quantum research have accelerated, and estimates for the arrival of practical quantum computing capabilities vary. Some experts predict that quantum computers capable of executing Shor's algorithm on relevant key sizes could emerge within the next 10 to 20 years, though significant engineering hurdles remain. This uncertainty makes it critical for DNSSEC stakeholders to begin preparing now, as cryptographic migrations of this scale require years of planning, testing, and phased rollouts.

The potential implications for national security, financial services, critical infrastructure, and internet stability make DNSSEC's resilience to quantum threats a global priority. Governments and regulatory bodies are increasingly incorporating quantum-readiness into cybersecurity strategies, recognizing that DNSSEC will be a crucial layer in safeguarding digital trust.

In parallel, efforts to develop hybrid cryptographic models are gaining traction. These models combine classical cryptographic algorithms with post-quantum algorithms in a complementary manner. Hybrid signatures could serve as an interim solution, enabling DNSSEC to benefit from the security of both algorithm classes while the global DNS infrastructure transitions to full post-quantum readiness. However, hybrid models will also increase DNS response sizes and require resolvers and authoritative servers to support additional complexity in signature verification processes.

Ultimately, DNSSEC's evolution in the era of quantum computing will involve a careful balance between adopting robust quantum-resistant cryptography and maintaining the operational and performance characteristics needed to keep DNS efficient and reliable. As organizations and DNS operators monitor advancements in quantum technology, proactive engagement in post-quantum planning will be key to ensuring that DNSSEC remains a trusted and vital component of global internet security for decades to come.

Future of DNS Security Protocols

The future of DNS security protocols is poised to evolve rapidly in response to growing cybersecurity threats, technological advancements, and the increasing demand for privacy and trust on the internet. The Domain Name System, which serves as the backbone of internet navigation, continues to face significant risks from a wide range of attack vectors, including cache poisoning, DNS spoofing, man-in-the-middle attacks, and data exfiltration. To address these challenges, the development and adoption of new DNS security protocols, as well as the enhancement of existing ones like DNSSEC, are essential to ensure a secure, resilient, and trustworthy DNS infrastructure for the digital age.

DNSSEC has long served as a cornerstone of DNS security by providing authenticity and integrity through cryptographic signatures. However, its scope does not include confidentiality. As internet users increasingly seek privacy in their online activities, attention has shifted to protocols that also provide protection against eavesdropping and data interception during DNS resolution. This demand has given rise to DNS-over-HTTPS (DoH) and DNS-over-TLS (DoT), two protocols that encrypt DNS queries and responses between clients and recursive resolvers. By leveraging standard encryption methods, DoH and DoT prevent intermediaries from viewing or altering DNS traffic, thereby addressing concerns about surveillance and censorship.

While DoH and DoT focus on encrypting the transport layer of DNS communication, they are often deployed in conjunction with DNSSEC to provide comprehensive security. DNSSEC ensures that DNS data has not been tampered with, while DoH and DoT secure the channel through which the data is transmitted. In the future, wider integration of these protocols will likely become the norm, especially as major browser vendors and operating systems continue to adopt DoH and DoT as default settings. This trend will require recursive resolvers to fully support encryption and validation, placing new performance and operational demands on DNS infrastructure providers.

Another significant area of innovation in DNS security is the development of Oblivious DNS-over-HTTPS (ODoH). ODoH is designed to enhance user privacy by introducing an additional layer of obfuscation. It separates the client's identity from the DNS query by routing encrypted DNS requests through an intermediary, or proxy, before reaching the resolver. This prevents any single entity from knowing both who made the request and what was requested. As privacy regulations tighten and user expectations evolve, protocols like ODoH are likely to gain traction, particularly in environments where anonymity and protection from tracking are paramount.

Looking ahead, the integration of DNS with decentralized technologies may also shape the future of DNS security. The concept of decentralized DNS, or D-DNS, utilizes blockchain and distributed ledger technology to create alternative domain name systems that are not reliant on centralized root servers. While still in experimental stages, these systems aim to provide censorship resistance and greater resilience against centralized failures or control. However, they face interoperability challenges and are not yet widely supported. As these systems mature, the possibility of integrating decentralized trust models with traditional DNSSEC frameworks may become a subject of exploration, offering a hybrid approach to DNS security.

Machine learning and artificial intelligence are also expected to play a growing role in DNS security. AI-driven anomaly detection systems can analyze DNS traffic in real time, identifying patterns that indicate malicious behavior, such as domain generation algorithms used by botnets or unusually high query volumes targeting specific zones. While these technologies do not replace DNSSEC or transport encryption, they serve as complementary tools for identifying and mitigating threats that exploit DNS infrastructure.

In the context of enterprise and critical infrastructure environments, DNS security protocols will increasingly be integrated into zero trust architectures. Zero trust assumes that all network traffic, including DNS queries, is potentially hostile and must be verified continuously. This paradigm shift will drive adoption of DNSSEC validation at the endpoint level, encrypted DNS transport, and strict access controls for DNS servers. Enterprises will need to deploy internal resolvers that enforce security policies while maintaining auditability and performance.

Emerging use cases, such as IoT and 5G networks, will demand DNS security protocols that can operate efficiently in resource-constrained and latency-sensitive environments. Efforts to optimize DNSSEC performance, reduce signature and key sizes, and improve resolver efficiency will be critical. Lightweight cryptographic algorithms and streamlined validation processes are being explored to make DNSSEC and encrypted DNS viable in these new contexts. Additionally, standardization bodies are considering ways to simplify DNSSEC deployment through automated key management and enhanced tooling.

Global policy and regulatory frameworks will also influence the future of DNS security. Governments and international organizations are beginning to recognize the strategic importance of DNS and the need for secure, resilient naming infrastructure. Policies mandating DNSSEC, encrypted DNS, and secure resolver practices are likely to emerge in more jurisdictions, particularly for public services, financial institutions, and sectors designated as critical infrastructure. Compliance requirements will drive broader adoption and standardization, accelerating the deployment of secure DNS protocols worldwide.

As quantum computing advances, the cryptographic algorithms underpinning DNSSEC will need to be replaced or supplemented with quantum-resistant alternatives. The transition to post-quantum cryptography represents a major milestone in the evolution of DNS security. Research is underway to identify suitable algorithms that balance security with performance, and future DNSSEC implementations will need to accommodate these changes through dual-algorithm approaches and new key management strategies.

Finally, user experience will remain a key consideration. For DNS security protocols to be successful, they must operate seamlessly, without introducing latency or complexity for end-users. Simplifying deployment for administrators, providing clear diagnostics, and ensuring compatibility across devices and networks will be critical to ensuring that DNS security evolves in a way that is both effective and accessible.

The future of DNS security protocols lies in the convergence of authentication, confidentiality, resilience, and privacy. By integrating DNSSEC with transport encryption, developing privacy-preserving technologies, and preparing for quantum threats, the internet community can build a DNS infrastructure that is secure, efficient, and future-proof. The continued evolution of DNS security protocols will be driven by collaboration among technologists, policymakers, and industry leaders, all working toward the shared goal of securing one of the internet's most fundamental systems.

DNSSEC and Cyber Threat Intelligence

DNSSEC and cyber threat intelligence are two critical pillars in modern cybersecurity that, when combined, offer organizations a powerful toolset to prevent, detect, and respond to DNS-based attacks. While DNSSEC focuses on ensuring the authenticity and integrity of DNS data through cryptographic signatures, cyber threat intelligence provides actionable insights about the tactics, techniques, and procedures used by adversaries. Together, these components enhance an organization's ability to defend against sophisticated attacks that target the DNS layer, which has long been exploited due to its historical lack of strong authentication mechanisms.

DNS-based attacks such as DNS cache poisoning, spoofing, and redirection campaigns are common tactics used by threat actors to manipulate DNS records, reroute users to malicious sites, or intercept sensitive data. Cybercriminals often use fake DNS responses to redirect traffic to phishing sites, command and control (C2) servers, or malware-hosting domains. DNSSEC mitigates these attacks by introducing digital signatures that allow resolvers to validate the authenticity of DNS responses. If a signature is missing or invalid, the resolver treats the response as bogus and prevents it from reaching the client, effectively stopping many DNS hijacking attempts before they cause damage.

Cyber threat intelligence teams play a crucial role in identifying emerging DNS-based threats and providing organizations with the knowledge needed to enhance DNSSEC deployments. Threat intelligence feeds regularly include indicators of compromise (IOCs) such as malicious domains, IP addresses, and DNS patterns linked to known threat actors or campaigns. Integrating this intelligence into DNSSEC-enabled environments enables organizations to enhance detection capabilities. For instance, when threat intelligence identifies new domains associated with malware distribution or phishing, security teams can proactively monitor DNSSEC validation logs to detect attempts to resolve these domains within the network.

DNSSEC validation data, when correlated with cyber threat intelligence, becomes a valuable source of situational awareness. Monitoring for validation failures, mismatches in DNSKEY or DS records, or unusual patterns of invalid DNS responses can provide early indicators of potential DNS manipulation attempts. Cyber threat intelligence teams can enrich these findings with context from ongoing campaigns or attack trends. For example, if a nation-state threat group is known to target financial institutions using DNS hijacking, sudden spikes in DNSSEC validation failures within a bank's network may warrant immediate investigation and escalation to incident response teams.

In environments where DNSSEC is implemented alongside security information and event management (SIEM) platforms, DNSSEC-related logs can be automatically enriched with threat intelligence data. This correlation allows security analysts to identify anomalies more quickly and determine whether they align with known threat actor behaviors. For instance, if a DNS query fails DNSSEC validation and simultaneously matches a domain on a threat intelligence blacklist, the system can generate a prioritized alert, enabling security teams to act swiftly.

DNSSEC also supports cyber threat intelligence by ensuring the integrity of DNS-based threat detection mechanisms. Many cybersecurity solutions rely on DNS queries and responses to detect malware communications, identify data exfiltration, or block access to known malicious domains. Without DNSSEC, these detection mechanisms can be undermined if an attacker successfully injects forged DNS responses or manipulates DNS traffic to evade monitoring. By securing the DNS resolution process, DNSSEC ensures that threat intelligence systems analyzing DNS logs or monitoring DNS traffic can trust the integrity of the data being processed.

The integration of DNSSEC into threat intelligence programs is particularly valuable in sectors such as government, finance, and healthcare, where the protection of sensitive data is paramount. Threat actors often use advanced DNS manipulation techniques as part of broader campaigns, and DNSSEC provides an essential defense layer against these sophisticated threats. Intelligence-sharing initiatives, such as Information Sharing and Analysis Centers (ISACs), also benefit from the visibility that DNSSEC provides. Organizations participating in these initiatives can contribute anonymized data on DNSSEC validation anomalies or observed attacks, strengthening the collective threat intelligence community.

Another emerging area is the use of DNSSEC data in machine learning models designed for threat detection. Security operations centers (SOCs) increasingly employ AI-driven platforms that analyze large volumes of network traffic, including DNS queries and responses, to detect abnormal behaviors. By feeding DNSSEC validation logs into these models, organizations can train algorithms to recognize patterns associated with DNS manipulation attempts, enriching the machine learning process with verified, high-integrity DNS data.

For cyber threat intelligence analysts, DNSSEC also presents opportunities to improve attribution efforts. By analyzing DNSSEC adoption patterns, key rollover behaviors, and signature anomalies, analysts may glean additional insights about the infrastructure used by threat actors. While DNSSEC primarily serves as a defensive control, its operational artifacts, such as DNSKEY rotation schedules and signature usage, can sometimes reveal the sophistication or operational maturity of adversaries attempting to exploit DNS weaknesses.

One of the operational challenges faced by organizations is ensuring that DNSSEC is implemented consistently across all zones and integrated into broader security ecosystems. Incomplete DNSSEC coverage, gaps in validation processes, or poor visibility into DNSSEC logs can limit the effectiveness of threat intelligence correlation. To address this, organizations must adopt a holistic approach that includes automating DNSSEC management, implementing rigorous validation at all recursive resolvers, and ensuring that DNSSEC-related logs are forwarded to SIEM platforms or threat intelligence platforms (TIPs) for enrichment and analysis.

As cyber threat landscapes evolve and adversaries develop more sophisticated DNS-based attack methods, the importance of DNSSEC and cyber threat intelligence will continue to grow. The future of this integration will likely involve the adoption of advanced telemetry solutions that provide deeper insights into DNSSEC validation events, anomaly detection, and automated threat hunting workflows based on real-time intelligence feeds.

DNSSEC serves as both a technical safeguard and a strategic enabler of effective cyber threat intelligence operations. By ensuring the trustworthiness of DNS data, DNSSEC empowers organizations to detect and disrupt DNS-level threats more effectively and to leverage threat intelligence for faster, more informed decision-making. The convergence of these two domains creates a security ecosystem where prevention, detection, and response processes are strengthened, reducing the likelihood of successful DNS-targeted attacks across diverse operational environments.

The Role of ICANN and IANA in DNSSEC

The successful deployment and operation of DNSSEC rely heavily on the efforts and governance provided by two key organizations: the Internet Corporation for Assigned Names and Numbers (ICANN) and the Internet Assigned Numbers Authority (IANA). Both play a critical role in maintaining the global DNS infrastructure and ensuring the security, stability, and resiliency of the internet's root zone, which is essential for DNSSEC to function properly across the internet. These organizations are central to managing the DNSSEC trust anchor, coordinating global key management processes, and supporting a consistent and secure DNSSEC implementation across the domain name ecosystem.

ICANN serves as the global nonprofit organization responsible for coordinating the maintenance and procedures of several databases related to the namespaces of the internet, most notably the Domain Name System. Its mission includes ensuring the stable and secure operation of the DNS, and one of its most visible functions is overseeing the global root zone. ICANN is responsible for accrediting domain registrars, facilitating policies among stakeholders, and coordinating technical operations that underpin internet stability. Within the context of DNSSEC, ICANN's role is crucial in managing the overall governance, communication, and multi-stakeholder collaboration necessary to ensure a unified and secure global DNSSEC deployment.

IANA, which is operated by ICANN, is tasked with managing the DNS root zone's key material, also known as the DNSSEC trust anchor. The root zone trust anchor is essentially the top-level cryptographic key that allows recursive resolvers and validating servers to authenticate DNSSEC signatures from the root zone downward through the DNS hierarchy. IANA generates and manages the Key Signing Key (KSK) used to sign the root zone's Zone Signing Key (ZSK), which in turn signs the root's resource records. This chain of cryptographic validation is what establishes the trust model for DNSSEC, enabling resolvers to verify that DNS responses originate from authoritative sources and have not been tampered with.

One of IANA's most significant responsibilities in DNSSEC operations is performing and managing the root KSK ceremonies. These ceremonies are highly controlled and meticulously documented events during which the cryptographic keys that sign the root zone's DNSKEY records are securely generated, stored, or rotated. These events are conducted under strict physical and procedural security measures to ensure transparency and trust within the global internet community. Participants in the ceremonies include representatives from ICANN, independent auditors, and trusted community representatives from different regions, all of whom serve as witnesses to reinforce the legitimacy of the process.

The transparency of the root KSK ceremonies is critical to reinforcing the global trust in DNSSEC. ICANN and IANA document each ceremony, record detailed logs, and make information about the key management process publicly available. The ceremonies are designed to be open to scrutiny, following well-defined and widely published procedures that provide assurance to stakeholders, including governments, corporations, and internet service providers, that the cryptographic keys securing the root zone are properly managed.

Another critical role of IANA under ICANN's oversight is the publication of the root zone trust anchor. The trust anchor, in the form of a DNSKEY record, is published on IANA's official website and in secure repositories, where network operators and software developers can retrieve it to configure validating resolvers and other DNSSEC-enabled systems. The trust anchor is essential for establishing the chain of trust from the root zone down to all other DNSSEC-protected zones on the internet.

ICANN also facilitates global policy development processes that impact DNSSEC deployment. Through the Internet Engineering Task Force (IETF) and other standards bodies, ICANN contributes to the technical evolution of DNSSEC, helping shape RFCs and best practices that affect DNSSEC operations worldwide. It plays an important role in stakeholder engagement, bringing together registries, registrars, ISPs, and security professionals to address interoperability challenges, operational concerns, and adoption barriers associated with DNSSEC.

ICANN's Root Zone Management partners include Verisign, which operates the root zone's authoritative servers and is responsible for generating and publishing the root zone file. Verisign and IANA work closely to ensure that DNSSEC-related changes, such as key rollovers, are coordinated and executed without disrupting global DNS resolution. The partnership ensures that the root zone's DNSSEC keys are correctly embedded within the zone file and that signed responses can be validated by recursive resolvers worldwide.

In 2017, ICANN and IANA executed the first-ever root KSK rollover, replacing the original KSK generated in 2010 with a new one. The KSK rollover process was a complex and highly visible event within the internet community, requiring extensive communication, testing, and phased implementation to minimize risks and disruptions. IANA played a pivotal role in coordinating this effort, from securely generating the new KSK during the root KSK ceremony to updating trust anchor repositories and guiding stakeholders through the transition. The successful rollover reinforced confidence in the resilience and flexibility of DNSSEC's trust model and demonstrated the ability of ICANN and IANA to manage cryptographic lifecycle events at the highest level of internet infrastructure.

ICANN also engages in outreach and education efforts to encourage DNSSEC adoption. It provides resources, training materials, and technical guidance to help DNS operators, registrars, and network administrators implement DNSSEC best practices. These initiatives are especially critical for countries and regions with developing internet infrastructure, where awareness of DNSSEC's benefits and operational requirements may still be limited.

Through its stewardship of IANA functions and its leadership in internet governance, ICANN ensures that DNSSEC continues to serve as a vital safeguard against DNS-related threats, such as spoofing and cache poisoning, which could undermine the integrity of internet communications. The collaboration between ICANN, IANA, root server operators, and the broader technical community plays a foundational role in maintaining the global trust that users place in the

DNS every day. By managing the DNSSEC trust anchor and upholding transparent, rigorous processes for key management, ICANN and IANA help ensure that the DNS remains a secure and reliable system for billions of users around the world.

DNSSEC in Open Source DNS Servers

DNSSEC has become an essential mechanism for ensuring the authenticity and integrity of DNS responses, and its adoption has been significantly facilitated by the availability and capabilities of open source DNS servers. Open source software plays a crucial role in the internet's infrastructure, offering transparency, flexibility, and innovation to organizations of all sizes. Within the realm of DNS, several open source DNS servers have been instrumental in promoting and enabling DNSSEC deployment. These servers provide both authoritative and recursive DNS services with built-in support for DNSSEC, allowing administrators to implement secure DNS resolution and zone signing without the need for proprietary software or costly licensing.

One of the most widely used open source DNS servers is BIND, developed and maintained by the Internet Systems Consortium (ISC). BIND has a long history in the DNS world and has been at the forefront of DNSSEC implementation. It provides comprehensive support for both DNSSEC signing and validation, making it suitable for use as an authoritative server that signs zones and as a recursive resolver that validates responses. BIND includes tools for key generation, such as dnssec-keygen, as well as mechanisms for key rollover and automated zone signing. Administrators can configure inline signing, where BIND dynamically signs zones on the fly, reducing the complexity of managing pre-signed zone files. For recursive resolver functionality, BIND supports DNSSEC validation by default, provided that the root trust anchor is configured. This enables BIND to authenticate DNS responses and reject any that fail validation, effectively mitigating DNS spoofing and cache poisoning attacks.

Another popular open source DNS server is Unbound, designed specifically as a recursive resolver with a strong focus on security and performance. Developed by NLnet Labs, Unbound is known for its efficient DNSSEC validation capabilities and its ability to operate in resource-constrained environments. It comes pre-configured with the root trust anchor and supports RFC 5011 automated trust anchor rollover, allowing it to maintain up-to-date trust relationships without manual intervention. Unbound also includes features such as DNS over TLS (DoT) and DNS over HTTPS (DoH), which can be combined with DNSSEC to provide both encryption and authentication of DNS data. Unbound's modular architecture and robust logging capabilities make it a popular choice for network operators who prioritize DNS security.

PowerDNS is another open source DNS server that supports both authoritative and recursive modes, with robust DNSSEC capabilities. As an authoritative server, PowerDNS allows zone signing using both offline and online methods. It supports integration with external key management systems, including Hardware Security Modules (HSMs), for enhanced protection of private keys. PowerDNS offers Lua scripting capabilities for custom DNS logic, and administrators can manage DNSSEC operations through a RESTful API, which facilitates automation and integration with DevOps workflows. As a recursive resolver, PowerDNS Recursor supports DNSSEC validation and can work alongside DNS filtering and policy enforcement tools, making it suitable for enterprise and ISP environments.

Knot DNS and Knot Resolver, developed by CZ.NIC, are modern open source DNS servers designed with high performance and DNSSEC support in mind. Knot DNS is an authoritative server that supports automatic zone signing, key management, and zone transfers with DNSSEC protection. Its focus on efficiency and scalability makes it ideal for large deployments requiring high query throughput. Knot Resolver, designed for recursive resolution, supports DNSSEC validation out of the box and is known for its fast query resolution times and flexible configuration. Both Knot DNS and Knot Resolver are used by several national registries and large-scale operators, reflecting their reliability and DNSSEC capabilities.

Open source DNS servers also provide important educational value for DNSSEC. Their transparency allows users and developers to study the implementation details of DNSSEC, understand the intricacies of the protocol, and contribute to its evolution. Community contributions help improve security, identify bugs, and optimize performance, fostering a collaborative environment that accelerates DNSSEC adoption. Documentation, tutorials, and community forums surrounding open source DNS software further lower the barrier to entry for organizations seeking to implement DNSSEC for the first time.

Despite the advantages, deploying DNSSEC with open source DNS servers requires careful planning and operational discipline. Administrators must manage cryptographic keys, ensure proper zone signing, monitor signature expiration, and handle key rollovers without disrupting service. Open source servers provide tools and automation options to facilitate these tasks, but the responsibility for correct configuration and ongoing maintenance lies with the operator. Failure to properly manage DNSSEC settings can result in validation failures, zone outages, or broken trust chains, underscoring the need for training and operational best practices.

To support administrators, many open source DNS servers offer integration with monitoring and alerting systems. They generate logs and metrics related to DNSSEC validation outcomes, signing operations, and key status, which can be fed into SIEM platforms or monitoring dashboards. These insights allow operators to detect issues such as signature expiration, validation anomalies, or DS record mismatches in real-time, enabling proactive management of DNSSEC infrastructure.

Open source DNS software also plays a critical role in testing and innovation. New DNSSEC features, cryptographic algorithms, and protocol enhancements are often implemented and validated in open source environments before being adopted more widely. For example, as the internet community prepares for the transition to post-quantum cryptography, open source DNS servers will be instrumental in testing and deploying quantum-resistant algorithms within DNSSEC. Their flexibility and openness allow rapid experimentation, ensuring that DNSSEC remains effective in the face of evolving security threats.

In summary, open source DNS servers are foundational to DNSSEC deployment worldwide. Their robust support for DNSSEC, coupled with community-driven development and transparency, empowers organizations to secure their DNS infrastructure cost-effectively and reliably. By providing tools for signing, validation, key management, and monitoring, these servers enable DNSSEC to be implemented at scale, reinforcing trust in DNS and strengthening the overall security of the internet. As DNS threats continue to grow in complexity, open source DNS servers will remain at the forefront of DNSSEC innovation, ensuring that secure name resolution remains accessible and effective for all.

DNSSEC and Third-Party DNS Services

The widespread adoption of third-party DNS services has significantly shaped how organizations and individuals manage and secure their DNS infrastructure. These services, provided by entities outside the organization such as cloud-based DNS providers, content delivery networks (CDNs), or managed DNS platforms, offer scalability, performance, and redundancy that might otherwise be difficult to achieve with self-hosted solutions. As the internet faces increasing threats to DNS infrastructure, integrating DNSSEC with third-party DNS services has become a critical consideration for ensuring the authenticity and integrity of DNS responses. However, leveraging DNSSEC in third-party DNS environments introduces unique benefits, dependencies, and operational challenges.

Third-party DNS services often provide authoritative DNS hosting, where they manage DNS zones and serve responses for customer domains. Many of these providers now include DNSSEC as part of their service offerings, allowing domain owners to sign their zones and establish a chain of trust to the DNS root. Major providers such as Cloudflare, Amazon Route 53, Google Cloud DNS, Akamai, and others have built DNSSEC capabilities into their platforms, making it easier for customers to adopt DNSSEC without needing to manage on-premises DNS servers. These providers typically offer automated zone signing, key generation, and key rollover processes, which simplifies the operational burden associated with DNSSEC deployment.

One of the primary advantages of using DNSSEC-enabled third-party DNS services is the automation and scalability they provide.

Traditional DNSSEC deployments often require significant manual intervention to manage cryptographic keys, sign zones, submit DS records to registrars, and monitor for signature expiration. Managed DNS providers abstract much of this complexity by providing user-friendly dashboards, APIs, and automation frameworks that streamline DNSSEC management. For organizations without deep DNSSEC expertise or dedicated network engineering resources, this automation lowers the barrier to adopting DNSSEC while maintaining a secure DNS infrastructure.

However, relying on third-party DNS services for DNSSEC also introduces certain trade-offs. By outsourcing DNSSEC operations, organizations cede some control over critical aspects of their DNS security posture, including key storage and rollover procedures. While reputable DNS providers adhere to strict security protocols and industry best practices, customers must trust that their provider's key management systems are sufficiently secure. This reliance on the provider's internal security controls, infrastructure resilience, and operational transparency requires careful vetting, as any compromise at the DNS provider level could undermine the trustworthiness of signed DNS zones.

Additionally, DNSSEC integration with third-party DNS services can vary in terms of flexibility and configurability. Some providers offer limited options for key algorithms or key sizes, restricting customers to a subset of supported cryptographic methods. For organizations with regulatory or internal security policies mandating specific cryptographic standards, this limitation could present compliance challenges. Furthermore, the level of customization available for DNSSEC-related records, such as DNSKEY and RRSIG TTLs or NSEC3 parameters, may differ between providers. These variations can impact how DNSSEC functions across different providers and may complicate multi-provider or hybrid DNS deployments.

Another consideration when using DNSSEC with third-party DNS services is the process of submitting Delegation Signer (DS) records to the parent zone through the domain registrar. While some DNS providers automate the submission of DS records for supported registrars, others require domain owners to manually retrieve DS records from the provider and input them into the registrar's interface.

This introduces the potential for human error, such as incorrect or incomplete DS record submissions, which can break the DNSSEC chain of trust. To mitigate this risk, organizations should maintain clear documentation and verification procedures when managing DS records in third-party DNS environments.

The integration of DNSSEC with third-party DNS services also impacts how organizations manage redundancy and failover. Many enterprises adopt multi-DNS or multi-CDN strategies to ensure availability and resilience against outages. In such architectures, DNS zones are hosted across multiple DNS providers, each serving as an authoritative source for the domain. Deploying DNSSEC in a multi-provider setup requires careful coordination to ensure that all providers sign zones with the same key material or compatible keys and that consistent DS records are published at the parent zone. Failing to align DNSSEC configurations across providers can result in inconsistent responses or validation failures for end-users.

Moreover, DNSSEC's impact on DNS response sizes and transport behaviors must be considered when using third-party DNS services. Signed zones generate larger responses due to additional records such as RRSIG and DNSKEY, which may affect how DNS queries traverse firewalls, load balancers, and resolvers that interact with the provider's infrastructure. While most reputable third-party DNS providers optimize their networks to handle large DNSSEC-enabled responses via EDNSo and fallback to TCP when necessary, customers must ensure that their own networks, including client-side resolvers, can accommodate the increased packet sizes and avoid truncation issues.

The role of DNSSEC in supporting broader security frameworks is also relevant when evaluating third-party DNS services. DNSSEC complements other security measures, such as TLS and email authentication protocols like DMARC, DKIM, and SPF. For instance, when used in conjunction with DANE (DNS-Based Authentication of Named Entities), DNSSEC provides an additional layer of protection by enabling the validation of TLSA records for securing TLS connections. Organizations that rely on third-party DNS services should ensure that their provider supports DNSSEC as a foundational element to enable these complementary security protocols effectively.

Transparency and reporting are key considerations when deploying DNSSEC through third-party DNS providers. Organizations must have access to detailed logs, metrics, and validation reports to monitor DNSSEC health, detect anomalies, and confirm compliance with security policies. Leading providers offer dashboards that display key DNSSEC statistics, including key rollover status, signature expiration timelines, and validation failure rates. Integration with external monitoring and alerting platforms, such as SIEM systems, further enhances the organization's ability to maintain visibility and respond proactively to DNSSEC-related issues.

In recent years, the growing focus on privacy and encryption has also influenced the evolution of third-party DNS services. Providers increasingly combine DNSSEC with encrypted DNS transport protocols such as DNS over TLS (DoT) and DNS over HTTPS (DoH). By delivering signed DNS data over encrypted channels, these providers help secure DNS traffic against tampering, spoofing, and passive surveillance. This convergence of DNSSEC and encrypted DNS further strengthens the end-to-end security posture of customers who depend on third-party DNS services for public-facing domains and critical infrastructure.

Ultimately, DNSSEC's role within third-party DNS services is to provide the assurance that DNS records have not been altered during transit and originate from authoritative sources. By leveraging managed DNS platforms with built-in DNSSEC support, organizations can improve their DNS security posture while benefiting from the performance and scalability offered by external providers. However, success in this model requires careful attention to provider capabilities, configuration consistency, and integration with broader security and monitoring frameworks to fully realize the benefits of a secure and resilient DNS infrastructure.

DNSSEC and Content Delivery Networks (CDNs)

The relationship between DNSSEC and Content Delivery Networks (CDNs) has become increasingly important as organizations seek to balance performance, availability, and security in delivering content to global audiences. CDNs play a pivotal role in accelerating web applications and websites by distributing content across geographically dispersed servers, thereby reducing latency and improving load times for end-users. As CDNs operate at the edge of the internet, they frequently interact with DNS to redirect user traffic to the nearest or most optimal edge server. However, integrating DNSSEC with CDN infrastructure introduces technical and operational considerations that require careful coordination.

A CDN typically relies on DNS-based load balancing to direct users to the most appropriate edge location. This is commonly implemented using authoritative DNS servers controlled by the CDN provider. When a user requests content hosted on a website using a CDN, the DNS query is answered by the CDN's authoritative servers, which provide a response directing the user to a nearby or less congested edge server. Given this reliance on DNS for traffic steering, securing these DNS responses is critical, as any manipulation of the responses could redirect users to unauthorized or malicious endpoints.

DNSSEC enhances the integrity of this process by ensuring that the DNS responses generated by a CDN's authoritative servers are cryptographically signed and verifiable. This prevents adversaries from injecting forged responses into the DNS resolution path, thereby mitigating risks such as cache poisoning, DNS hijacking, or man-in-the-middle attacks that could compromise user traffic. However, the deployment of DNSSEC in a CDN environment is more complex than in traditional static DNS hosting scenarios due to the dynamic and distributed nature of CDNs.

One of the key challenges lies in DNSSEC's dependence on pre-signed records. In traditional DNSSEC implementations, authoritative servers sign static zone files in advance, generating RRSIG records that are distributed along with DNS responses. CDNs, by contrast, often generate DNS responses dynamically based on real-time network conditions, user location, or traffic patterns. This means that the CDN must have mechanisms in place to dynamically sign DNS responses or to pre-sign responses for multiple permutations of possible queries and responses.

To address this challenge, leading CDN providers have implemented DNSSEC support within their DNS infrastructure, enabling the automatic signing of responses at the edge. Providers like Cloudflare, Akamai, Fastly, and others offer DNSSEC signing services for their customers, allowing zones to be signed as part of the CDN's managed DNS platform. The CDN's authoritative servers handle the signing process and manage key material on behalf of their customers, simplifying DNSSEC adoption for organizations using the CDN's DNS infrastructure.

While this approach provides operational efficiency, it also raises questions around trust and key management. When a customer relies on a CDN to sign its DNS zones, the CDN controls the private keys used to generate DNSSEC signatures. This requires customers to trust that the CDN follows strict security protocols for key generation, storage, and rotation. For organizations operating in regulated environments or with strict internal security policies, this reliance on the CDN for key management may require additional due diligence or contractual assurances.

The coordination between a customer's domain registrar, the CDN, and the parent zone operator is also essential. When enabling DNSSEC with a CDN, customers must publish the appropriate Delegation Signer (DS) record at the registrar level to link the zone's DNSSEC key material to the DNSSEC chain of trust. CDNs typically provide the necessary DNSKEY or DS records for this purpose, but the process of updating the registrar records remains a critical step that customers must execute carefully to avoid disrupting DNS resolution or breaking the trust chain.

Another consideration is the potential performance impact of DNSSEC in CDN environments. DNSSEC increases the size of DNS responses due to the addition of RRSIG, DNSKEY, and other related records. Larger DNS responses may lead to UDP packet truncation and trigger fallback to TCP, introducing additional latency in the DNS resolution process. This is particularly relevant for CDNs, where fast DNS resolution is critical to minimizing page load times and providing optimal user experience. To mitigate this, CDNs optimize their networks and DNS configurations to handle large DNS responses efficiently, including support for EDNS0 and the adjustment of maximum UDP payload sizes.

DNSSEC in CDN environments also interacts with other security and performance-enhancing technologies. Many CDN providers support TLS encryption and HTTP/3 at the edge, and DNSSEC complements these layers by securing the initial DNS resolution step. Additionally, DNSSEC can be integrated with DNS over HTTPS (DoH) or DNS over TLS (DoT) to provide both encryption and authenticity for DNS traffic. In such configurations, DNS queries and responses are encrypted during transport while still benefiting from the cryptographic guarantees provided by DNSSEC.

A further layer of complexity arises in multi-CDN deployments, where organizations leverage two or more CDN providers to increase redundancy and geographic coverage. In these cases, DNSSEC deployment requires careful alignment of key management, zone signing, and DS record publication across all CDN providers to ensure consistency. Any discrepancies between DNSSEC implementations across different CDNs can result in validation failures or inconsistent DNS behavior for end-users. Organizations deploying multi-CDN strategies must coordinate closely with all CDN vendors to maintain a unified DNSSEC configuration.

Monitoring and troubleshooting DNSSEC in a CDN context also require specialized tools and processes. Given that DNS responses may be signed at multiple edge locations, variations in cache states, key usage, or resolver behavior across geographic regions must be accounted for. CDN providers typically offer logging and monitoring features that allow customers to track DNSSEC signing operations, key rollovers, and validation statistics. Integrating these logs into centralized security monitoring platforms enables organizations to maintain visibility over DNSSEC operations and respond quickly to anomalies.

Despite the complexities, the combination of DNSSEC and CDN services provides a powerful defense against a range of DNS-layer attacks while supporting global content delivery at scale. As attackers continue to target the DNS infrastructure to launch phishing campaigns, credential theft, and data interception, securing the DNS layer with DNSSEC becomes essential. For organizations relying on CDNs to serve content to global audiences, DNSSEC ensures that the redirection mechanisms used to steer users to edge servers are protected against tampering.

In an increasingly interconnected world, where speed, availability, and security must coexist, DNSSEC within CDN environments serves as a cornerstone of modern internet resilience. By securing the DNS layer while leveraging the performance benefits of CDN infrastructure, organizations can provide a faster and safer online experience for users worldwide. The future will likely see continued collaboration between CDN providers and the DNSSEC community to further streamline deployment, enhance automation, and address emerging challenges, ensuring that DNSSEC remains a critical component of secure global content delivery.

Legal and Regulatory Aspects of DNSSEC

The implementation of DNSSEC has significant legal and regulatory implications as it directly affects the security and integrity of critical internet infrastructure. DNSSEC was designed as a technical solution to protect against DNS-based attacks by providing authentication of DNS data, but its adoption intersects with several domains of law, including cybersecurity regulation, data protection, compliance frameworks, and contractual obligations. As organizations increasingly rely on DNSSEC to secure their online presence, understanding the legal and regulatory landscape surrounding DNSSEC becomes essential for decision-makers and network administrators.

One of the most prominent regulatory drivers influencing DNSSEC adoption is the growing number of national and international cybersecurity laws mandating the protection of critical information infrastructure. In many jurisdictions, the DNS is classified as critical infrastructure due to its role in enabling essential services such as financial transactions, government communications, healthcare delivery, and public safety systems. Regulations such as the European Union's NIS Directive (Directive on Security of Network and Information Systems) require operators of essential services and digital service providers to implement security measures that ensure the availability and integrity of critical services. While the directive does not explicitly mandate DNSSEC, its emphasis on preventing DNS-based attacks encourages the use of DNSSEC as part of a broader risk management and mitigation strategy.

Similarly, regulatory bodies in the United States have issued guidance and policies aimed at improving DNS security. The Federal Risk and Authorization Management Program (FedRAMP) and the Office of Management and Budget (OMB) have required federal agencies to deploy DNSSEC on publicly accessible federal government domains. The Department of Homeland Security (DHS) has also issued binding operational directives that mandate DNSSEC implementation within certain governmental networks. These mandates underscore DNSSEC's role as a regulatory expectation for securing public sector systems, and other jurisdictions have taken similar steps to require DNSSEC within governmental and public-facing infrastructure.

In addition to regulatory mandates, contractual obligations between organizations and their partners, customers, or service providers may reference DNSSEC as a best practice or required control. For example, managed DNS service contracts, cloud hosting agreements, and domain registrar terms of service may stipulate that DNSSEC be implemented to fulfill security and service-level commitments. In the financial sector, contractual agreements with regulators or partners may require DNSSEC adoption as part of broader requirements to safeguard financial transactions and customer data against DNS tampering or redirection attacks.

DNSSEC is also relevant in the context of data protection laws. Although DNSSEC itself does not encrypt data or provide confidentiality, it plays a crucial role in preventing unauthorized manipulation of DNS responses that could lead to the interception or compromise of personal data. Under regulations such as the General Data Protection Regulation (GDPR) in the European Union or the

California Consumer Privacy Act (CCPA) in the United States, organizations are required to implement appropriate technical and organizational measures to protect personal data against unauthorized access or disclosure. Since DNSSEC can prevent attackers from rerouting users to phishing websites or fraudulent domains that could harvest personal data, its deployment may be seen as an important component of meeting these data protection obligations.

The legal implications of DNSSEC extend to liability and due diligence considerations. Organizations that operate online platforms or critical services may face legal liability if a failure to implement reasonable security measures, such as DNSSEC, results in harm to customers or third parties. Courts and regulators may assess whether an organization followed industry best practices, which increasingly include DNSSEC as a recommended or expected control for DNS security. In the event of a security incident related to DNS manipulation, the absence of DNSSEC could be viewed as a failure to exercise due care, exposing the organization to legal claims or regulatory penalties.

Another legal dimension relates to the role of domain registrars and top-level domain registries in enabling DNSSEC. Registrars that fail to support DNSSEC services, such as facilitating the submission of Delegation Signer (DS) records, may face scrutiny under consumer protection laws if their limitations expose customers to unnecessary risks. Furthermore, registries operating under national regulations may be required to offer DNSSEC capabilities to domain registrants, especially in ccTLDs where governments maintain direct oversight of the registry's policies and operations.

International treaties and cooperative agreements among nations also influence the regulatory landscape for DNSSEC. Initiatives led by organizations such as the International Telecommunication Union (ITU) and regional bodies like the European Union Agency for Cybersecurity (ENISA) promote DNSSEC as part of national and international cybersecurity strategies. While these initiatives may not have the force of law, they shape the expectations of governments and industry stakeholders regarding the minimum security standards for DNS infrastructure.

Export control laws can also play a role, albeit indirectly, in DNSSEC deployment. DNSSEC relies on cryptographic algorithms and technologies that are subject to export regulations in certain countries. While common algorithms like RSA and SHA-256 are generally classified as mass-market encryption under export regulations such as the U.S. Export Administration Regulations (EAR), organizations operating internationally must ensure compliance with relevant export control laws when deploying DNSSEC-related technologies across borders.

An additional regulatory consideration involves transparency and accountability in DNSSEC operations. Governments and industry bodies expect organizations implementing DNSSEC to maintain records of key management activities, such as the generation, storage, rollover, and destruction of cryptographic keys. This aligns with broader regulatory requirements for auditability and incident response preparedness, particularly in sectors such as finance, healthcare, and telecommunications.

Finally, the emergence of quantum computing raises forward-looking regulatory questions about the future of DNSSEC. As regulators anticipate the potential for quantum computers to break current cryptographic algorithms, guidance on transitioning to post-quantum cryptography will increasingly affect DNSSEC operations. Organizations may be required to demonstrate proactive planning and risk mitigation strategies related to DNSSEC's cryptographic resilience, with regulators monitoring industry readiness for adopting quantum-safe algorithms.

In this evolving landscape, organizations must treat DNSSEC not only as a technical control but also as a component of their legal and regulatory compliance strategy. By understanding the legal expectations and aligning DNSSEC deployment with applicable laws and contractual requirements, organizations can strengthen their cybersecurity defenses, reduce legal exposure, and enhance trust with stakeholders who rely on the integrity and availability of their digital services. The role of DNSSEC will continue to expand as regulators, industry standards bodies, and international frameworks increasingly emphasize the importance of securing the global DNS infrastructure against emerging threats.

Educating Stakeholders About DNSSEC

Educating stakeholders about DNSSEC is a fundamental component of successful implementation and adoption. Despite its technical significance in securing the Domain Name System, DNSSEC often suffers from a lack of awareness or understanding among key decision-makers, technical teams, and non-technical stakeholders alike. As DNSSEC affects a wide range of organizational functions, from IT operations and cybersecurity to legal compliance and customer trust, it is crucial to develop tailored education strategies that effectively communicate its value and operational requirements to different audiences.

The first step in educating stakeholders is identifying the various groups that will interact with or be affected by DNSSEC. Technical teams, including DNS administrators, network engineers, and cybersecurity professionals, need in-depth knowledge of DNSSEC protocols, cryptographic operations, key management, and troubleshooting techniques. These teams are responsible for deploying, configuring, and maintaining DNSSEC within the organization's infrastructure. Their training should focus on the practical aspects of DNSSEC, including generating DNSKEY and RRSIG records, managing key rollovers, publishing DS records with registrars, and validating DNSSEC-enabled queries on recursive resolvers. Workshops, hands-on labs, and formal training courses are effective methods for equipping technical teams with the expertise required to manage DNSSEC reliably.

Beyond technical staff, educating executive leadership and non-technical stakeholders about DNSSEC is equally important. Executives and decision-makers may not need to understand the granular details of cryptographic operations but should be informed about how DNSSEC enhances the security posture of the organization. They need to recognize DNSSEC as a critical control that protects against DNS-based attacks, such as cache poisoning and domain hijacking, which could otherwise undermine the availability and integrity of web applications, online services, and internal networks. Framing DNSSEC as part of a larger risk management and compliance strategy helps to secure executive buy-in and justify budget allocations for DNSSEC-related projects.

Legal and compliance teams also play a role in DNSSEC adoption. Educating these stakeholders involves highlighting how DNSSEC aligns with regulatory requirements and contractual obligations for protecting critical infrastructure and customer data. Legal teams should understand that DNSSEC supports the integrity of internet transactions by ensuring that users resolve to legitimate domains. Explaining how DNSSEC complements data protection laws and cybersecurity frameworks, such as GDPR, NIS2 Directive, or sector-specific regulations in finance and healthcare, enables compliance teams to incorporate DNSSEC into internal policies and audit checklists.

End-user education, while not as common for DNSSEC as for other security measures like multi-factor authentication, is still relevant in certain contexts. In organizations where employees are responsible for managing subdomains or overseeing third-party services, it is important to raise awareness about DNSSEC's purpose and benefits. For example, marketing and product teams managing customer-facing websites should understand that DNSSEC can contribute to securing brand reputation by preventing users from being redirected to fraudulent domains through DNS tampering. Basic education for non-technical staff can be delivered through awareness campaigns, newsletters, or brief training sessions that explain DNSSEC's role in maintaining customer trust and securing digital services.

A key challenge in DNSSEC education is demystifying its complexity. DNSSEC involves concepts such as asymmetric cryptography, digital signatures, trust chains, and secure delegation, which can be difficult for non-specialists to grasp. To overcome this barrier, educational materials should present DNSSEC in plain language, using visual aids, analogies, and real-world scenarios to illustrate its value. For instance, explaining DNSSEC as a digital signature for DNS responses that verifies the authenticity of information received from authoritative servers helps make the concept relatable to audiences less familiar with cybersecurity.

Cross-departmental collaboration is also essential to successful DNSSEC education. DNSSEC deployment touches multiple teams, including IT, security, legal, procurement, and even communications teams that handle public messaging. Facilitating joint workshops, tabletop exercises, and cross-functional working groups helps ensure that all relevant stakeholders are aligned on DNSSEC goals, responsibilities, and operational requirements. Such collaboration fosters a shared understanding of how DNSSEC impacts various business functions and promotes organizational readiness.

Another critical aspect of stakeholder education is addressing misconceptions and concerns about DNSSEC. Some stakeholders may perceive DNSSEC as a burdensome or overly technical initiative that offers limited return on investment. Others may worry about potential performance impacts, such as increased DNS response sizes or resolver latency due to DNSSEC validation. Educational efforts should acknowledge these concerns while providing evidence-based insights. For example, explaining how modern DNS infrastructure supports larger DNS responses through EDNS0, or how DNSSEC can reduce the risk of costly security incidents, can help counter objections and promote informed decision-making.

Real-world case studies are valuable tools for illustrating the importance of DNSSEC to stakeholders. Highlighting incidents where organizations fell victim to DNS spoofing or cache poisoning due to the absence of DNSSEC demonstrates the tangible consequences of insecure DNS infrastructure. Conversely, showcasing success stories where DNSSEC deployment protected an organization from attacks or strengthened compliance with regulatory mandates provides positive reinforcement and practical examples of DNSSEC's benefits.

DNSSEC education should also address the evolving threat landscape. As cyber threats targeting the DNS layer become more sophisticated, including DNS tunneling, man-in-the-middle attacks, and targeted DNS hijacking campaigns, stakeholders must understand how DNSSEC serves as a foundational layer of defense against these threats. By framing DNSSEC as part of a broader defense-in-depth strategy that complements other security controls, such as TLS, DANE, or encrypted DNS transport protocols, educators can present a holistic view of DNS security.

Finally, continuous learning and knowledge sharing are crucial for maintaining DNSSEC awareness over time. DNSSEC is not a set-it-and-forget-it solution. It requires ongoing monitoring, key rollovers, incident response planning, and adaptation to new standards or cryptographic recommendations. Organizations should establish internal knowledge bases, conduct periodic refresher trainings, and participate in external forums, such as DNS-OARC or ICANN workshops, to stay current with DNSSEC developments and best practices.

Educating stakeholders about DNSSEC is a long-term commitment that strengthens both technical implementation and organizational resilience. By fostering a culture of awareness and collaboration, organizations can maximize the effectiveness of DNSSEC, protect their DNS infrastructure, and contribute to the broader security and stability of the internet.

DNSSEC in Academic Research

DNSSEC has been a subject of continuous interest in academic research due to its critical role in strengthening the security of the Domain Name System. Academic institutions, cybersecurity researchers, and technical communities have examined DNSSEC from a wide range of perspectives, including its cryptographic foundations, operational challenges, deployment trends, and its interaction with other emerging internet protocols. The findings and contributions from these research efforts have played a vital role in shaping the evolution of DNSSEC and informing best practices for its implementation across diverse environments.

One significant focus area in academic research is the study of DNSSEC deployment patterns and adoption rates across the internet. Researchers have used large-scale data collection and measurement methodologies to assess how widely DNSSEC has been deployed by top-level domains (TLDs), second-level domains, and critical infrastructure providers. These studies often reveal disparities in deployment levels, showing that while certain regions or industries have embraced DNSSEC, others continue to lag behind. Such research has been instrumental in identifying barriers to adoption, including technical complexity, limited awareness, or economic constraints that hinder broader DNSSEC uptake.

Another key area of academic exploration involves the cryptographic algorithms used in DNSSEC. Scholars have examined the efficiency, resilience, and computational overhead of algorithms like RSA and ECDSA in DNSSEC signing and validation processes. These studies have provided insights into the trade-offs between security and performance, influencing recommendations for algorithm selection. More recently, academic research has shifted toward investigating quantum-resistant cryptographic algorithms suitable for DNSSEC, anticipating the potential threat posed by the advent of quantum computing. This research has contributed to discussions within standardization bodies such as the IETF and has informed experimental efforts to integrate post-quantum cryptography into DNSSEC prototypes.

DNSSEC's impact on network performance and system scalability has also been a central theme in academic studies. Researchers have analyzed the effects of DNSSEC on DNS response sizes, resolver latency, and packet loss rates in various network environments. These findings have shed light on how DNSSEC-related overhead can influence user experience and network resource consumption, particularly in environments with limited bandwidth or legacy infrastructure. Such research has led to the development of optimization techniques, including resolver-side caching strategies, signature minimization, and enhancements to DNS transport protocols, such as EDNSo, that help mitigate the performance impacts of DNSSEC.

In addition to performance considerations, academic researchers have explored DNSSEC's role in mitigating specific security threats. Empirical studies have evaluated how effectively DNSSEC prevents common DNS attacks such as cache poisoning, spoofing, and man-in-the-middle interception. By analyzing data from real-world attack campaigns and simulated environments, researchers have validated DNSSEC's ability to protect against tampering with DNS responses. These findings have reinforced the understanding that DNSSEC serves as a foundational control in protecting the DNS layer, while also emphasizing that DNSSEC must be implemented alongside other security measures, such as TLS, to achieve comprehensive protection.

Academic research has also contributed to understanding the human factors influencing DNSSEC deployment. Studies focusing on operator behavior, usability, and decision-making have examined why some organizations choose to adopt DNSSEC while others do not. These investigations often highlight a lack of training, limited incentives, and organizational inertia as significant barriers. By identifying these challenges, researchers have advocated for educational initiatives, streamlined tooling, and policy interventions to support wider DNSSEC adoption.

DNSSEC's interaction with other protocols has generated significant research interest. For instance, the integration of DNSSEC with DANE (DNS-based Authentication of Named Entities) for securing TLS connections has been the subject of both theoretical and applied studies. Researchers have assessed the security benefits and operational challenges of deploying DNSSEC-enabled DANE for services such as email (via SMTP) and web servers. Additionally, research on DNSSEC in conjunction with DNS privacy protocols like DNS-over-HTTPS (DoH) and DNS-over-TLS (DoT) has examined how these protocols can complement each other to provide both confidentiality and authenticity for DNS queries and responses.

Another growing area of research explores the role of DNSSEC in emerging network architectures, including edge computing, IoT ecosystems, and software-defined networking (SDN). In these contexts, researchers have explored how DNSSEC can be adapted to secure dynamic and decentralized environments where traditional DNS architectures may not be directly applicable. For example, studies have proposed mechanisms for efficiently implementing DNSSEC in IoT networks with constrained devices, addressing the challenges posed by limited computational power and network resources.

Research on DNSSEC has also extended into the realm of policy and governance. Scholars have analyzed the global policy frameworks that shape DNSSEC deployment, including the role of ICANN, national governments, and international bodies. These studies often highlight how geopolitical considerations, legal mandates, and industry regulations influence the rate and scope of DNSSEC adoption in different parts of the world. By exploring these dynamics, researchers contribute to discussions on how to harmonize DNSSEC deployment with broader internet governance principles.

Finally, the academic community has contributed valuable tools and frameworks for testing and monitoring DNSSEC implementations. Open-source software, such as DNSSEC diagnostic tools, validation platforms, and measurement frameworks, often originates from research projects conducted in universities or technical institutes. These tools are widely used by DNS operators, service providers, and security analysts to verify DNSSEC configurations, diagnose validation failures, and monitor trust chain health across DNS infrastructures.

Through these varied research efforts, academic institutions continue to play a pivotal role in advancing the understanding, implementation, and evolution of DNSSEC. Their work not only addresses technical challenges but also explores the organizational, regulatory, and socio-economic factors influencing DNSSEC adoption worldwide. As the internet evolves and new threats emerge, ongoing academic research into DNSSEC will remain essential for refining the protocol, informing best practices, and ensuring the security and resilience of the DNS as a critical component of global internet infrastructure.

The Future of DNSSEC and Beyond

The future of DNSSEC is closely tied to the evolving landscape of internet security, technological innovation, and emerging cyber threats. As organizations and users increasingly demand stronger protection for their digital communications, DNSSEC is expected to play an even more prominent role in the coming years. However, the evolution of DNSSEC will also be shaped by its integration with new technologies, operational enhancements, and complementary protocols that address the broader spectrum of DNS-related vulnerabilities and performance considerations.

One of the most anticipated developments influencing DNSSEC's future is the emergence of quantum computing. The current cryptographic algorithms used by DNSSEC, such as RSA and ECDSA, are vulnerable to the theoretical capabilities of quantum computers running Shor's algorithm. As quantum computing progresses from research labs to practical applications, the cryptography community is actively preparing for the transition to post-quantum cryptographic (PQC) algorithms. For DNSSEC, this transition will require the adoption of quantum-resistant key algorithms that can safeguard DNS integrity against future quantum attacks. Efforts by standardization bodies like NIST and the IETF are already underway to identify and recommend PQC algorithms suitable for DNSSEC and other internet protocols.

Beyond cryptographic resilience, automation will be key to DNSSEC's growth. While DNSSEC adoption has steadily increased, it remains uneven across industries and regions due to perceived operational complexity. Advances in automation for key generation, rollover, and zone signing processes will reduce administrative overhead and eliminate common misconfigurations. Modern DNS platforms, both open-source and commercial, are integrating automation features such as automatic DS record updates with registrars and intelligent key management systems that improve DNSSEC's usability and reliability.

The convergence of DNSSEC with privacy-enhancing technologies is another factor shaping its future. As internet users and regulators place greater emphasis on data privacy, DNS-over-HTTPS (DoH) and DNS-over-TLS (DoT) are increasingly being deployed to encrypt DNS queries in transit. When combined with DNSSEC, these protocols provide end-to-end security for DNS transactions, delivering both confidentiality and data integrity. Future deployments are likely to feature DNSSEC and encrypted DNS as standard, especially in critical environments such as financial services, healthcare, and government networks where the security of name resolution is paramount.

In the broader security ecosystem, DNSSEC's role will expand beyond its traditional focus on preventing cache poisoning and response forgery. Its integration with DANE, for example, provides a framework for binding TLS certificates to domain names via DNS, reducing reliance on the public certificate authority (CA) system and strengthening the trust model for internet communications. Widespread adoption of DANE in conjunction with DNSSEC could help mitigate risks associated with CA compromises and improve the security of TLS connections across the web and other internet services.

DNSSEC will also play a crucial role in securing the growing number of IoT devices and edge computing environments. These networks often rely on DNS to resolve service endpoints, update configurations, and communicate with cloud services. As IoT ecosystems continue to expand, ensuring the authenticity of DNS responses is critical to preventing unauthorized device redirection or malicious firmware updates. Future research and standards development will likely focus on lightweight DNSSEC models optimized for constrained devices and decentralized network architectures.

Another emerging trend is the development of decentralized DNS alternatives based on blockchain and distributed ledger technologies. While these systems propose to eliminate centralized control points in DNS, they still require mechanisms to verify the authenticity and integrity of records. Elements of DNSSEC's trust model, such as cryptographic signatures and hierarchical trust chains, may influence or be integrated into decentralized DNS frameworks, creating hybrid systems that blend traditional and blockchain-based naming infrastructures.

The evolution of DNSSEC will also involve deeper integration with security automation and threat intelligence platforms. By correlating DNSSEC validation data with real-time threat intelligence feeds, organizations can enhance their ability to detect anomalies such as rogue DNS responses, misconfigurations, or indicators of attack campaigns targeting the DNS layer. Automation will enable faster incident response by flagging and remediating DNSSEC-related security issues, contributing to a more resilient and responsive DNS security posture.

Operational best practices and education will continue to be key factors in shaping DNSSEC's adoption and effectiveness. As awareness of DNSSEC's benefits spreads, organizations will increasingly integrate DNSSEC into their overall security strategies. Industry-specific guidance, regulatory frameworks, and supply chain requirements are expected to drive further adoption in sectors such as critical infrastructure, defense, and telecommunications.

Ultimately, the future of DNSSEC will be defined by its ability to evolve in response to new technological paradigms, threats, and user expectations. Its role as a foundational security control will continue to expand as it intersects with next-generation internet protocols and architectures, ensuring that DNS remains a secure and trustworthy component of the global digital ecosystem.

www.ingramcontent.com/pod-product-compliance
Lightning Source LLC
LaVergne TN
LVHW051238050326
832903LV00028B/2455

* 9 7 9 8 3 1 5 2 9 0 6 0 5 *